Enrichment Workbook

STRETCH YOUR THINKING

TEACHER'S EDITION
Grade 6

Harcourt Brace & Company

Orlando • Atlanta • Austin • Boston • San Francisco • Chicago • Dallas • New York • Toronto • London

http://www.hbschool.com

CONTENTS

Riddle Fun

Match each number written in words in Column 1 with its standard
form in Column 2. Then write each corresponding letter on the line
below marked with the exercise number. You will not use every letter
to solve the riddle.

Column 1

Column 2

1. two thousand and six tenths __L__

2. three million, seventeen __O__

3. forty-six and eight thousandths __A__

4. five hundred fourteen thousand and nine tenths __M__

5. twelve million and fifty thousandths __B__

6. six hundred twenty-one ten-thousandths __U__

7. two thousand six ten-thousandths __C__

8. one million and one hundredth __T__

9. forty-six ten-thousandths __E__

10. five hundred nine ten-thousandths __Y__

11. twelve million, fifty thousand __N__

12. six hundred thousand, twenty-one __H__

A. 46.008
B. 12,000,000.050
C. 0.2006
E. 0.0046
H. 600,021
L. 2,000.6
M. 514,000.9
N. 12,050,000
O. 3,000,017
T. 1,000,000.01
U. 0.0621
Y. 0.0509

What did one number say to another number?

Y	O	U		C	A	N		C	O	U	N	T
10	2	6		7	3	11		7	2	6	11	8

O	N		M	E
2	11		4	9

STRETCH YOUR THINKING   E1

Comparing Scoring Leaders

SCORING LEADERS	
Player	**Average**
Rick Barry	24.8
Elgin Baylor	27.4
Wilt Chamberlain	30.1
George Gervin	25.1
Bob Pettit	26.4
Oscar Robertson	25.7
Jerry West	27.0

The table above shows the scoring averages of some retired NBA scoring leaders. Use the table to answer the questions.

1. Which of the players listed in the table has the greatest average?

   Wilt Chamberlain

2. Which of the players listed in the table has the lowest average?

   Rick Barry

3. Use > to list the averages of Oscar Robertson, George Gervin, and Bob Pettit from greatest to least.

   26.4 > 25.7 > 25.1

4. Use < to list all the averages shown in the table from least to greatest.

   24.8 < 25.1 < 25.7 < 26.4 < 27.0 < 27.4 < 30.1

5. Dominique Wilkins's scoring average was 26.5. Where would he be placed in the list you made in Exercise 4?

   after Bob Pettit (26.4) but before Jerry West (27.0)

6. Michael Jordan's scoring average was 32.3. Where would he be placed in the list you made in Exercise 4?

   after Wilt Chamberlain (30.1)

7. Which player in the table had an average greater than 25.5 but less than 26.0?

   Oscar Robertson

8. Which players in the table had an average greater than 26 but less than 28?

   Elgin Baylor, Bob Pettit, Jerry West

E2 STRETCH YOUR THINKING

Name ___________________________

Decimal Patterns

Find the next three terms in the pattern. Then write the rule for the pattern.

1. $\frac{1}{5}$, $\frac{2}{5}$, $\frac{3}{5}$, $\frac{4}{5}$, $\frac{5}{5}$, $\frac{6}{5}$, $\frac{7}{5}$, $\frac{8}{5}$, $\frac{9}{5}$

0.20   0.40   0.60   0.80   1.00   1.20   **1.40**   **1.60**   **1.80**

Add $\frac{1}{5}$ (0.20) to previous number.

Rule: ___________________________

2. $\frac{11}{2}$, $\frac{10}{2}$, $\frac{9}{2}$, $\frac{8}{2}$, $\frac{7}{2}$, $\frac{6}{2}$, $\frac{5}{2}$, $\frac{4}{2}$, $\frac{3}{2}$

5.5   5.0   4.5   4.0   3.5   3.0   **2.5**   **2.0**   **1.5**

Subtract $\frac{1}{2}$ (0.5) from previous number.

Rule: ___________________________

3. $\frac{3}{10}$, $\frac{6}{10}$, $\frac{9}{10}$, $\frac{12}{10}$, $\frac{15}{10}$, $\frac{18}{10}$, $\frac{21}{10}$, $\frac{24}{10}$, $\frac{27}{10}$

0.3   0.6   0.9   1.2   1.5   1.8   **2.1**   **2.4**   **2.7**

Add $\frac{3}{10}$ (0.3) to previous number.

Rule: ___________________________

4. $\frac{25}{4}$, $\frac{24}{4}$, $\frac{23}{4}$, $\frac{22}{4}$, $\frac{21}{4}$, $\frac{20}{4}$, $\frac{19}{4}$, $\frac{18}{4}$, $\frac{17}{4}$

6.25   6.00   5.75   5.50   5.25   5.00   **4.75**   **4.50**   **4.25**

Subtract $\frac{1}{4}$ (0.25) from previous number.

Rule: ___________________________

5. $\frac{44}{10}$, $\frac{40}{10}$, $\frac{36}{10}$, $\frac{32}{10}$, $\frac{28}{10}$, $\frac{24}{10}$, $\frac{20}{10}$, $\frac{16}{10}$, $\frac{12}{10}$, $\frac{8}{10}$

4.4   4.0   3.6   3.2   2.8   2.4   2.0   **1.6**   **1.2**   **0.8**

Subtract $\frac{4}{10}$ (0.4) from previous number.

Rule: ___________________________

6. $\frac{99}{100}$, $\frac{88}{100}$, $\frac{77}{100}$, $\frac{66}{100}$, $\frac{55}{100}$, $\frac{44}{100}$, $\frac{33}{100}$, $\frac{22}{100}$

0.99   0.88   0.77   0.66   0.55   **0.44**   **0.33**   **0.22**

Subtract $\frac{11}{100}$ (0.11) from previous number.

Rule: ___________________________

STRETCH YOUR THINKING   E3

Puzzling Exponents

Complete the puzzle with the values.

Across

1. 11^3
2. 5^3
3. 17^2
4. 7^4
5. 14^3
6. 9^4
7. 5^5
8. 10^4
9. 16^2
10. 2^7
11. 15^3

Down

1. 25^3
3. 6^3
8. 30^2
10. 6^4
12. 2^{10}
13. 7^3
14. 20^2
15. 12^3
16. 24^2
17. 3^7

Name That Floor

The floor selection keys found in a hotel's elevator are shown. Each of the following describes a ride in the elevator.

Use integers to show how each rider's position changed. Then name the floor on which each person left the elevator. The first one is done for you.

(14)
(13)
(12)
(11)
(10)
(9)
(8)
(7)
(6)
(5)
(4)
(3)
(2)
(1)
(M) Mezzanine
(L) Lobby
(G) Garage

1. Sue entered the elevator on the seventh floor. She traveled up three floors and then down five floors before leaving the elevator.

+3; −5; fifth floor

2. Josh entered the elevator at the lobby. He went up six floors and then down two before leaving the elevator.

+6; −2; third floor

3. Rob got on the elevator on the twelfth floor. He rode down to the mezzanine and then up four floors before leaving the elevator.

−12, +4; fourth floor

4. Tim entered the elevator from the garage. He rode up eight floors, down two floors, and then up another three floors before exiting.

+8, −2, +3; seventh floor

5. Jon entered the elevator on the ninth floor. He rode up five floors, down six floors, and then down another two floors before leaving the elevator.

+5, −6, −2; sixth floor

6. Tina got on the elevator at the lobby. She rode up to the fourteenth floor, down six floors, up four floors, and then she exited the elevator.

+15, −6, +4; twelfth floor

7. Evan entered the elevator on the fifth floor. He rode down to the mezzanine, down to the garage, and up four floors before leaving.

−5, −2, +4; second floor

8. Carole got on the elevator on the first floor. She rode up six floors, down to the mezzanine, and then up two floors before exiting.

+6, −7, +2; second floor

Investigating the House of Representatives

The legislative branch of government has two houses, the Senate and
the House of Representatives. Each state has two senators. However,
the population of a state determines how many representatives are
sent to the House of Representatives. The larger the population of the
state, the greater the number of representatives.

The table below shows the number of representatives various states
sent to the House. Use the table to answer the questions below.

State	Number of Representatives	State	Number of Representatives
Alabama	7	Michigan	16
Alaska	1	New Jersey	13
Arizona	6	New York	31
California	52	North Carolina	12
Colorado	6	Ohio	19
Florida	23	Oregon	5
Georgia	11	Pennsylvania	21
Hawaii	2	Rhode Island	2
Illinois	20	Texas	30
Indiana	10	Utah	3
Kansas	4	Virginia	11
Louisiana	7	Wisconsin	9

1. How many representatives in all do the states
    of Florida, Michigan, and Virginia have? _________ **50**

2. How many representatives in all do the states of
    North Carolina, New Jersey, and Pennsylvania have? _________ **46**

3. Which two states send the greatest number of
    representatives? What is their combined total? **California and New York; 83**

4. Which three states send the fewest representatives?
    What is their combined total? **Alaska, Hawaii, Rhode Island; 5**

5. How many representatives are sent from states
    with names that begin with a vowel? **71**

6. Find two pairs of states with a representative total of 50. Then find

    three states with the same total. **Illinois and Texas or New York and Ohio;**

    Florida, Michigan, and Virginia or Indiana, Ohio, and Pennsylvania

Patterns, Patterns

Draw the next three figures of the pattern. Then describe the rule used to form the pattern.

1.

Rule: **Triangle, square, then repeat adding one triangle and one square, repeating**

2.

Rule: **Circle, square, diamond, then reverse**

3.

Rule: **Circle, diamond, circle, then replace circles with squares, then back to circle, diamond, circle, repeating**

4.

Rule: **Square 1/4 shaded, square 1/2 shaded, square entirely shaded, then reverse**

Give the next three numbers in the pattern. Then describe the rule.

5. 1, 2, 4, 8, 16, 32, **64**, **128**, **256**, . . .

Rule: **Multiply by 2.**

6. 3, 2, 4, 3, 5, 4, **6**, **5**, **7**, . . .

Rule: **Subtract 1, add 2.**

7. 3, 6, 9, 15, 24, 39, **63**, **102**, **165**, . . .

Rule: **Add the two previous terms.**

STRETCH YOUR THINKING   E7

Solve It

Use mental math to solve each problem in the Decoder Box. Find the product in the Tip Box. Each time the product appears, write the letter of that problem above it. When you have solved all the problems, you will discover the math tip.

Decoder Box

A $2 \times 9 \times 5 =$	**90**	**N** $13 \times 3 \times 2 =$	**78**
B $7 \times 14 =$	**98**	**O** $4 \times 11 \times 3 =$	**132**
C $120 \times 4 =$	**480**	**P** $9 \times 22 =$	**198**
D $6 \times 7 \times 10 =$	**420**	**Q** $5 \times 34 \times 4 =$	**680**
E $55 \times 3 =$	**165**	**R** $15 \times 4 \times 2 =$	**120**
F $6 \times 8 \times 5 =$	**240**	**S** $16 \times 7 =$	**112**
H $2 \times 13 \times 5 =$	**130**	**T** $25 \times 6 =$	**150**
I $7 \times 21 =$	**147**	**U** $88 \times 5 =$	**440**
K $29 \times 8 =$	**232**	**V** $25 \times 19 \times 4 =$	**1,900**
L $9 \times 2 \times 6 =$	**108**	**Y** $7 \times 8 \times 5 =$	**280**
M $8 \times 5 \times 4 =$	**160**	**Z** $9 \times 53 =$	**477**

Tip Box

F	A	C	T	O	R	S		C	A	N		B	E
240	90	480	150	132	120	112		480	90	78		98	165

M	U	L	T	I	P	L	I	E	D		I	N
160	440	108	150	147	198	108	147	165	420		147	78

A	N	Y		O	R	D	E	R
90	78	280		132	120	420	165	120

Now use the Decoder Box to help you find the answer to a riddle.

What is only useful when it's used up?

A	N		U	M	B	R	E	L	L	A
90	78		440	160	98	120	165	108	108	90

E8   STRETCH YOUR THINKING

Number Crossword

Solve each problem. Complete the puzzle with the answers.

Across

1. $1,685 \times 124 =$ _____ **208,940**

2. $65 \times 104 =$ _____ **6,760**

3. $2,549 \times 317 =$ _____ **808,033**

4. $596 \times 240 =$ _____ **143,040**

5. $99 \times 5 =$ _____ **495**

6. $6,058 \times 847 =$ _____ **5,131,126**

7. $351 \times 208 =$ _____ **73,008**

8. $872 \times 234 =$ _____ **204,048**

Down

1. $6,150 \div 3 =$ _____ **2,050**

4. $3,454 \div 22 =$ _____ **157**

5. $855 \div 19 =$ _____ **45**

9. $25,344 \div 36 =$ _____ **704**

10. $16,740 \div 54 =$ _____ **310**

11. $7,968 \div 16 =$ _____ **498**

12. $46,295 \div 47 =$ _____ **985**

13. $17,568 \div 36 =$ _____ **488**

14. $14,761 \div 29 =$ _____ **509**

15. $32,625 \div 87 =$ _____ **375**

16. $9,672 \div 93 =$ _____ **104**

17. $7,896 \div 12 =$ _____ **658**

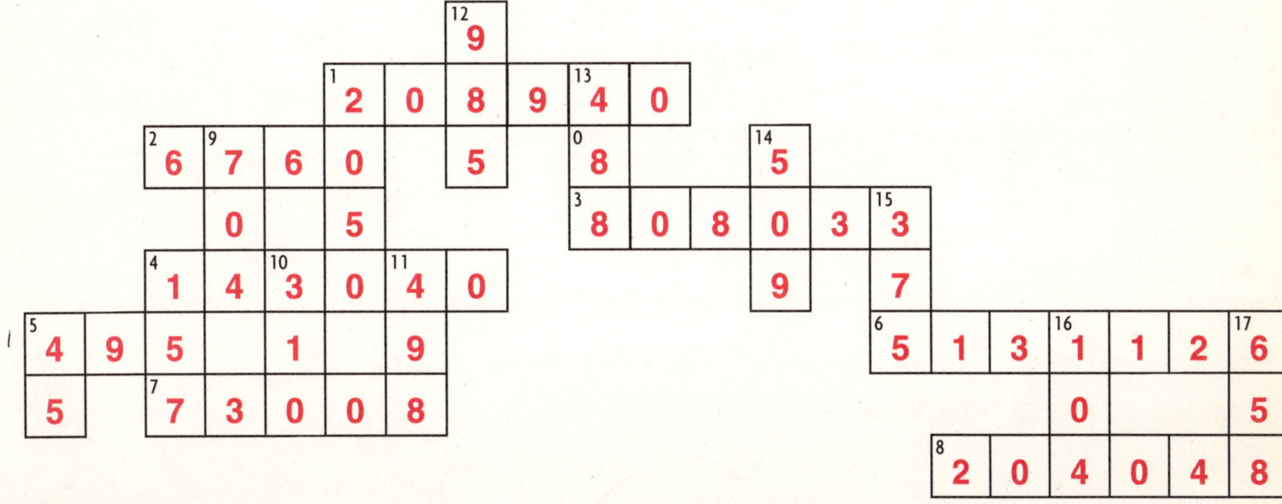

Estimating Populations

POPULATION OF THE MIDDLE COLONIES: 1670 – 1750					
Colony	1670	1690	1710	1730	1750
Delaware	700	1,482	3,645	9,170	28,704
New Jersey	1,000	8,000	19,872	35,510	71,393
New York	5,754	13,909	21,625	48,594	76,696
Pennsylvania	—	11,450	24,450	51,707	119,666

The table shows how the population of the middle colonies changed from 1670 to 1750. Use the table to answer the questions. Estimate to the nearest thousand.

1. About how many people lived in either Delaware or New York in 1690?

   about 15,000 people

2. About how many people lived in either Pennsylvania or New Jersey in 1730?

   about 88,000 people

3. About how many more people lived in New York than in Delaware in 1710?

   about 18,000 more people

4. About how many more people lived in Pennsylvania in 1750 than in 1690?

   about 109,000 more people

5. About how many people lived in the middle colonies in 1670?

   about 8,000 people

6. About how many people lived in the middle colonies in 1750?

   about 297,000 people

7. About how many more people lived in the middle colonies in 1750 than in 1670?

   about 289,000 more people

Shopping at the School Store

<table>
<tr><td colspan="4">SALE FLYER</td></tr>
<tr><td>Bookcover</td><td>$0.25</td><td>Note Cards</td><td>$0.98</td></tr>
<tr><td>Eraser</td><td>$0.15</td><td>Pen</td><td>$0.79</td></tr>
<tr><td>Paper</td><td>$1.89</td><td>Set of Markers</td><td>$3.95</td></tr>
<tr><td>Gym Shorts</td><td>$4.59</td><td>School Sweatshirt</td><td>$14.79</td></tr>
<tr><td>Highlighter</td><td>$1.29</td><td>School T-shirt</td><td>$5.98</td></tr>
</table>

The Heartsville School Store is having a back-to-school sale. Use the sale flyer above to solve.

1. Alana bought five different items. The total cost was $13.09. What were the items?

    bookcover, note cards, highlighter, school T-shirt, and gym shorts

2. Zack bought two items. The total cost was more than $25, but less than $30. What did he buy? How much did he spend?

    2 school sweatshirts; $29.58

3. Rico bought 2 each of three different items. They cost $2.38. What were the items?

    pens, erasers, and bookcovers

4. Adam spent $11.22 for four different items. What did he buy?

    pen, paper, set of markers, and gym shorts

5. Lonnie spent more than $5.00 but less than $5.50 on six different items. What did Lonnie buy?

    eraser, pen, bookcover, note cards, paper, and highlighter

6. Donna bought 3 each of two different items. She spent a total of $3.69. What did Donna buy?

    bookcovers and note cards

7. Name two combinations of five items. Each combination should have a total cost greater than $3, but less than $4. You may include more than one of some items.

    Possible answers: 1 bookcover, 2 erasers, 1 paper, 1 highlighter; 3 pens, 1 note cards, 1 bookcover

8. Name two combinations of four different items. Each combination should have a total cost greater than $16, but less than $20.

    Possible answers: school sweatshirt, gym shorts, bookcover, and eraser; gym shorts, school T-shirt, set of markers, and paper

STRETCH YOUR THINKING   E11

Pattern Practice

Identify the subtraction rule that was used to create each pattern. Then name the next three decimals.

1. 94.8, 94.3, 92.8, 90.3, __**86.8**__, __**82.3**__, __**76.8**__ . . .

   Rule: __**Subtract 0.5, then 1.5, then 2.5, and so on.**__

2. 78.26, 77.15, 74.93, 71.6, __**67.16**__, __**61.61**__, __**54.95**__ . . .

   Rule: __**Subtract 1.11, then 2.22, then 3.33, and so on.**__

3. 52.3, 50.2, 48, 45.7, __**43.3**__, __**40.8**__, __**38.2**__ . . .

   Rule: __**Subtract 2.1, then 2.2, then 2.3, then 2.4, and so on.**__

4. 27.5, 26, 23.5, 22, __**19.5**__, __**18**__, __**15.5**__ . . .

   Rule: __**Subtract 1.5, then 2.5, then 1.5, and so on.**__

5. 64.23, 58.53, 53.73, 48.03, __**43.23**__, __**37.53**__, __**32.73**__ . . .

   Rule: __**Subtract 5.7, then 4.8, then 5.7, and so on.**__

6. 103.26, 93.27, 84.39, 76.62, __**69.96**__, __**64.41**__, __**59.97**__ . . .

   Rule: __**Subtract 9.99, then 8.88, then 7.77, and so on.**__

7. 815.634, 803.289, 748.968, 736.623, __**682.302**__, __**669.957**__, __**615.636**__ . . .

   Rule: __**Subtract 12.345, then 54.321, then 12.345, and so on.**__

8. 128.003, 121.757, 113.558, 107.312, __**99.113**__, __**92.867**__, __**84.668**__ . . .

   Rule: __**Subtract 6.246, then 8.199, then 6.246, and so on.**__

9. 38.15, 35.25, 29.85, 26.95, __**21.55**__, __**18.65**__, __**13.25**__ . . .

   Rule: __**Subtract 2.9, then 5.4, then 2.9, and so on.**__

10. Make up two pattern problems of your own. Exchange papers with a classmate and solve. **Check students' work.**

____

____

Puzzling Problems

Find each product. Locate the product in the Tip Box. (Hint: Not all products are in the Tip Box.)

Each time the product appears, write the letter of that exercise above it. When you have solved all the problems, you will discover a math tip for multiplying decimals.

A	$5.26 \times 7.5 =$	**39.45**	**N**	$2.008 \times 1.2 =$	**2.4096**
B	$0.12 \times 1.2 =$	**0.144**	**O**	$6.1 \times 0.42 =$	**2.562**
C	$3 \times 0.009 =$	**0.027**	**P**	$0.54 \times 2.9 =$	**1.566**
D	$2.9 \times 2.03 =$	**5.887**	**R**	$0.3 \times 30 =$	**9**
E	$8 \times 2.5 =$	**20**	**S**	$1.8 \times 2.3 =$	**4.14**
G	$0.15 \times 0.07 =$	**0.0105**	**T**	$6 \times 1.7 =$	**10.2**
H	$7.4 \times 6.8 =$	**50.32**	**U**	$5.9 \times 0.04 =$	**0.236**
I	$0.04 \times 40.5 =$	**1.62**	**V**	$8.5 \times 6.3 =$	**53.55**
J	$0.25 \times 3.8 =$	**0.95**	**W**	$46.7 \times 2.3 =$	**107.41**
M	$190 \times 0.03 =$	**5.7**			

Tip Box

R	**E**	**M**	**E**	**M**	**B**	**E**	**R**		
9	20	5.7	20	5.7	0.144	20	9		

T	**O**		**E**	**S**	**T**	**I**	**M**	**A**	**T**	**E**
10.2	2.562		20	4.14	10.2	1.62	5.7	39.45	10.2	20

T	**H**	**E**		**P**	**R**	**O**	**D**	**U**	**C**	**T**
10.2	50.32	20		1.566	9	2.562	5.887	0.236	0.027	10.2

Decimal Solutions

Find each quotient. Locate the quotient in the Tip Box. (Hint: Not all quotients are in the Tip Box.)
Each time the quotient appears, write the letter of that exercise above it. When you have solved all the problems, you will discover a math tip for dividing decimals.

A	$6.3 \div 0.05 =$	126	**N**	$9.3 \div 0.6 =$	15.5
B	$50.2 \div 0.01 =$	5,020	**O**	$0.0024 \div 0.3 =$	0.008
C	$33.6 \div 8 =$	4.2	**P**	$8.7 \div 17.4 =$	0.5
E	$5.4 \div 0.02 =$	270	**Q**	$28.7 \div 8.2 =$	3.5
F	$107.91 \div 5.5 =$	19.62	**R**	$400.98 \div 24.6 =$	16.3
G	$4.077 \div 0.18 =$	22.65	**S**	$21.54 \div 0.6 =$	35.9
H	$9 \div 0.3 =$	30	**T**	$0.4168 \div 8 =$	0.0521
I	$1.6 \div 0.4 =$	4	**U**	$25 \div 0.005 =$	5,000
K	$5.44 \div 1.7 =$	3.2	**W**	$0.568 \div 0.4 =$	1.42
L	$0.192 \div 0.3 =$	0.64	**Y**	$4.48 \div 0.08 =$	56
M	$8.05 \div 0.7 =$	11.5	**Z**	$6.3 \div 0.18 =$	35

Tip Box

M	U	L	T	I	P	L	Y		T	O
11.5	5,000	0.64	0.0521	4	0.5	0.64	56		0.0521	0.008

C	H	E	C	K		T	H	E
4.2	30	270	4.2	3.2		0.0521	30	270

A	N	S	W	E	R
126	15.5	35.9	1.42	270	16.3

 STRETCH YOUR THINKING

Pyramid Power

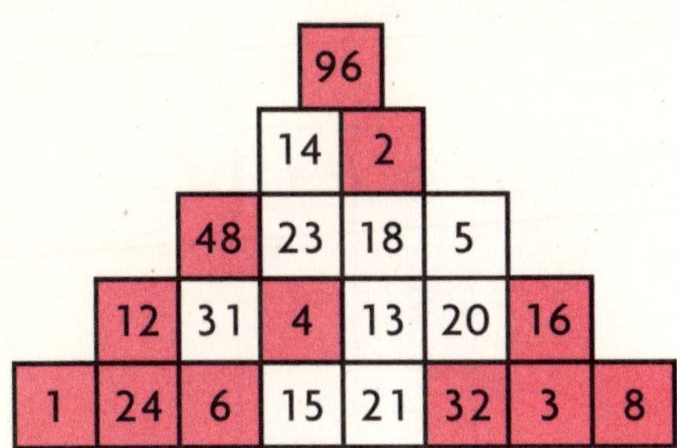

1. Shade the boxes that contain factors of 96.

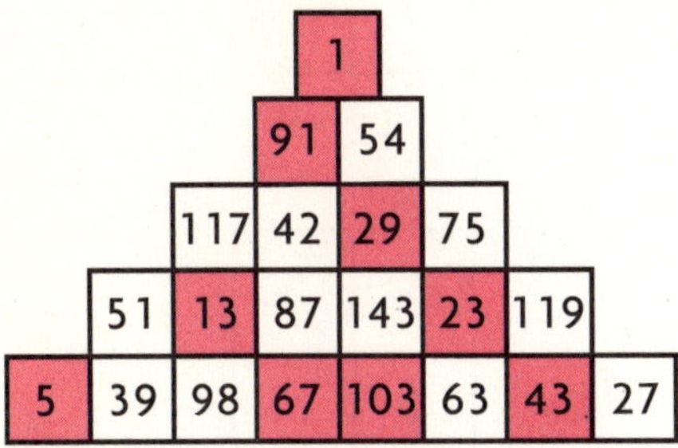

2. Shade the boxes that contain prime numbers.

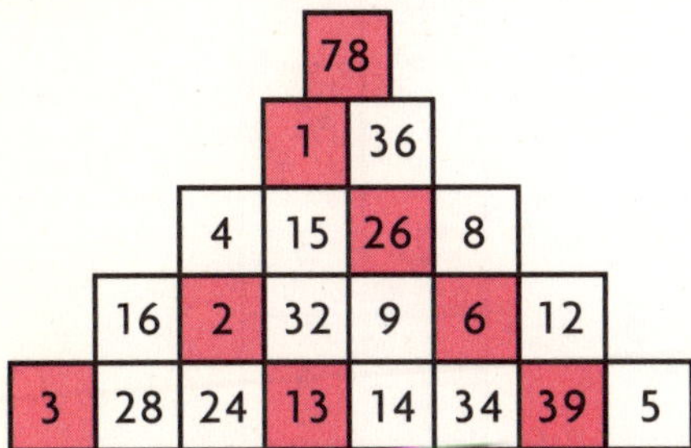

3. Shade the boxes that contain factors of 78.

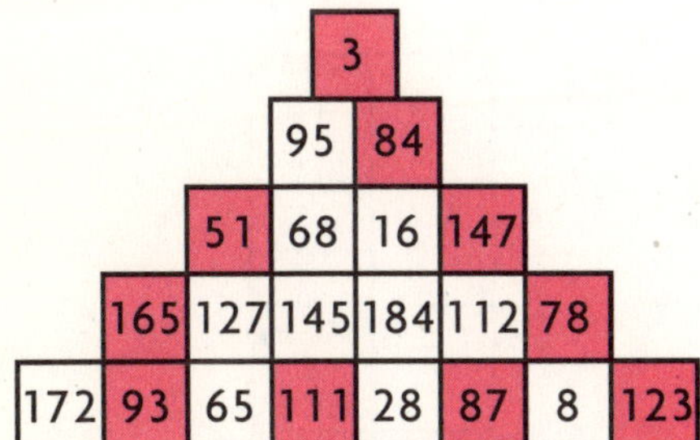

4. Shade the boxes that contain multiples of 3.

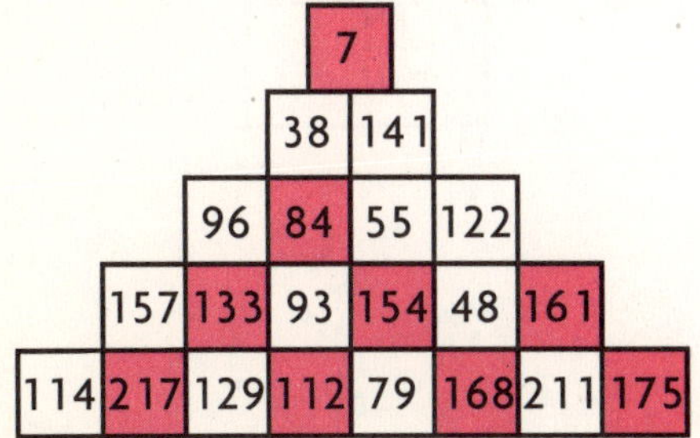

5. Shade the boxes that contain multiples of 7.

STRETCH YOUR THINKING   E15

Figure the Prime Factors

Shade one box in each row to show the prime factors of the given number.

1. 84

7	2
2	3
11	2
2	5

2. 225

5	3
5	2
3	7
2	3

3. 56

2	7
2	3
5	2
3	2

4. 144

7	3
3	5
3	2
11	2
2	5
2	7

5. 234

3	13
7	3
2	3
5	2

6. 96

5	3
2	11
2	5
7	2
2	3
2	5

7. 208

13	2
11	2
2	5
2	3
2	5

8. 340

17	13
5	7
3	2
2	11

9. 456

17	19
11	3
7	2
3	2
2	5

Multiple Relationships

Fill in each blank with a number from the box below. Then, identify the relationship described. The first two are done for you. You will not use every number in the box.

108	62	~~42~~	8	~~51~~	19	120	36
180	95	9	15	16	310	192	25
75	30	94	60	27	64	~~12~~	35

1. 17 is to __51__ and 85 as 19 is to 57 and 95. What is the relationship?
17 is the GCF of 51 and 85; 19 is the GCF of 57 and 95

2. __42__ is to 6 and 14 as 48 is to __12__ and 16. What is the relationship?
42 is the LCM of 6 and 14; 48 is the LCM of 12 and 16

3. 45 is to __9__ and 15 as 120 is to 24 and 30. What is the relationship?

45 is the LCM of 9 and 15; 120 is the LCM of 24 and 30

4. 36 is to 108 and 180 as __64__ is to 192 and 320. What is the relationship?

36 is the GCF of 108 and 180; 64 is the GCF of 192 and 320

5. 47 is to 94 and 235 as 62 is to 124 and __310__. What is the relationship?

47 is the GCF of 94 and 235; 62 is the GCF of 124 and 310

6. 105 is to 15 and 35 as __108__ is to 12 and 27. What is the relationship?

105 is the LCM of 15 and 35; 108 is the LCM of 12 and 27

7. 12 is to 24 and 36 as __25__ is to 50 and 75. What is the relationship?

12 is the GCF of 24 and 36; 25 is the GCF of 50 and 75

Fraction Flowers

Shade each petal that contains a fraction in simplest form.
Then write the other fractions in simplest form.

1.

2.

3.

4.

5.

6.

7.

8.

9.

10.

E18   STRETCH YOUR THINKING

Fraction Squares

Shade the squares that show fractions equivalent to the mixed number in the center.

1.

$\frac{93}{31}$	$\frac{41}{6}$	$\frac{30}{12}$
$\frac{35}{14}$	$2\frac{1}{2}$	$\frac{20}{12}$
$\frac{65}{26}$	$\frac{37}{13}$	$\frac{10}{4}$

2.

$\frac{24}{7}$	$\frac{143}{39}$	$\frac{121}{33}$
$\frac{45}{14}$	$3\frac{2}{3}$	$\frac{110}{30}$
$\frac{66}{18}$	$\frac{95}{26}$	$\frac{36}{12}$

3.

$\frac{242}{55}$	$\frac{18}{4}$	$\frac{21}{5}$
$\frac{286}{65}$	$4\frac{2}{5}$	$\frac{250}{75}$
$\frac{168}{32}$	$\frac{154}{35}$	$\frac{220}{50}$

4.

$\frac{96}{18}$	$\frac{336}{64}$	$\frac{126}{14}$
$\frac{105}{20}$	$5\frac{1}{4}$	$\frac{63}{12}$
$\frac{252}{48}$	$\frac{210}{40}$	$\frac{122}{24}$

5.

$\frac{340}{50}$	$\frac{98}{13}$	$\frac{220}{33}$
$\frac{140}{21}$	$6\frac{2}{3}$	$\frac{160}{32}$
$\frac{320}{48}$	$\frac{100}{15}$	$\frac{450}{45}$

6.

$\frac{105}{10}$	$\frac{17}{3}$	$\frac{43}{4}$
$\frac{42}{4}$	$10\frac{1}{2}$	$\frac{872}{119}$
$\frac{420}{40}$	$\frac{84}{8}$	$\frac{273}{26}$

Minute Math

There are 60 minutes in 1 hour. In the grid at the right, each square represents one minute, so the entire grid represents one hour.

Write the fraction of an hour. Then tell how many minutes there are.

1. Divide the grid into 5 equal parts. Shade one part.

   This represents $\dfrac{1}{5}$ of an hour. How many

   minutes is that? **12 min**

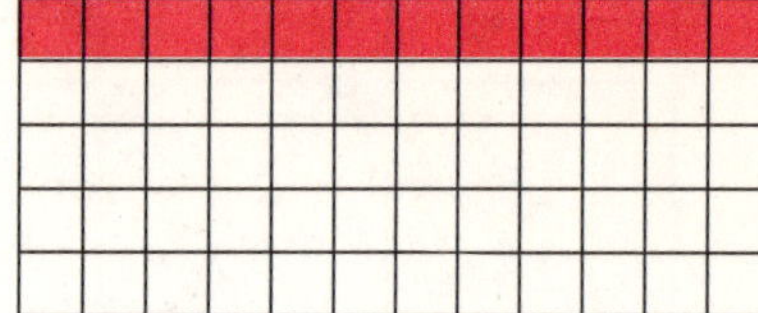

2. Divide the grid into 4 equal parts. Shade one part.

   How many minutes is that? **15 min**

3. Divide the grid into 3 equal parts. Shade one part.

   This represents $\dfrac{1}{3}$ of an hour. How many

   minutes is that? **20 min**

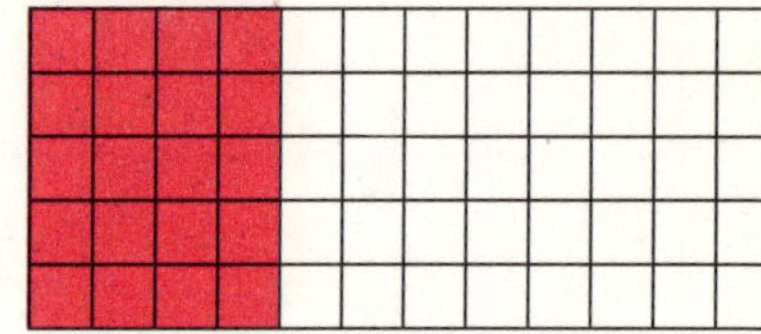

4. Divide the grid into 2 equal parts. Shade one part.

   This represents $\dfrac{1}{2}$ of an hour. How many

   minutes is that? **30 min**

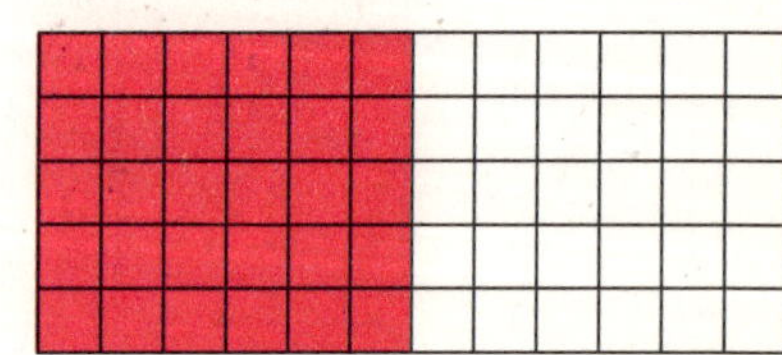

Solve. Draw grids and shade them if it helps you.

5. Rick exercised for $\frac{2}{3}$ hr. Then he read a book for $\frac{2}{5}$ hr. How much total time did Rick spend exercising and reading?

   1 hr and 4 min

6. Bella spent $\frac{1}{2}$ hr shopping. Then she spent $\frac{4}{5}$ hr cooking dinner. How much total time did Bella spend shopping and cooking?

   1 hr and 18 min

7. Jon played golf for $\frac{2}{3}$ hr. Then he spent $\frac{1}{2}$ hr talking with some friends. How much total time did he spend playing golf and talking?

   1 hr and 10 min

8. Ronnie jogged for $\frac{3}{5}$ hr. Then she listened to music for $\frac{2}{3}$ hr. How much total time did Ronnie jog and listen to music?

   1 hr and 16 min

E20   STRETCH YOUR THINKING

Geometric Fractions

Each figure below is a fractional part of the square shown at the right.

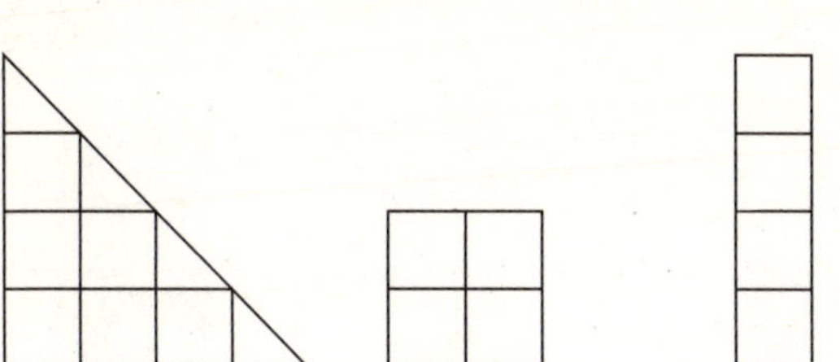 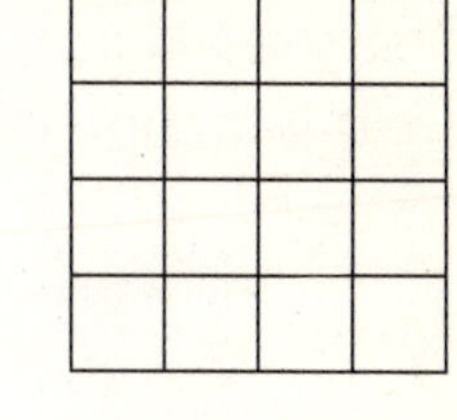

Figure 1   Figure 2   Figure 3   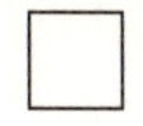 Figure 4   Figure 5   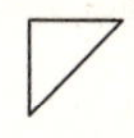 Figure 6

Write a fraction that identifies the part of the square represented by the figure. Then tell how many of the figures are needed to make one whole square. The first one has been done for you.

1. Figure 1 _$\frac{1}{2}$; two large triangles_

2. Figure 2 $\frac{1}{4}$; four small squares

3. Figure 3 $\frac{1}{4}$; four small rectangles

4. Figure 4 $\frac{1}{8}$; eight small rectangles

5. Figure 5 $\frac{1}{16}$; sixteen small squares

6. Figure 6 $\frac{1}{32}$; thirty-two small triangles

Now look at the figures below and the large rectangle at the right. Follow the same directions as above.

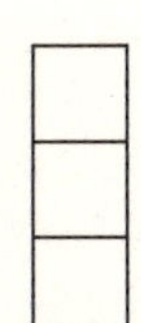 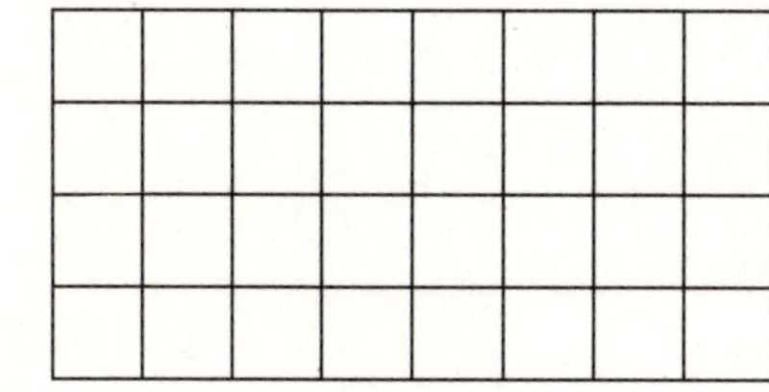 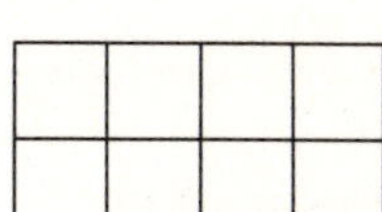 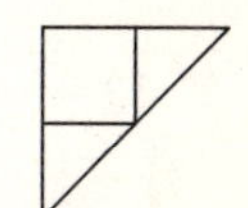

Figure 7   Figure 8   Figure 9   Figure 10

7. Figure 7 $\frac{1}{16}$; sixteen small rectangles

8. Figure 8 $\frac{2}{3}$; one and one-half small rectangles

9. Figure 9 $\frac{1}{6}$; six small rectangles

10. Figure 10 $\frac{1}{24}$; twenty-four small triangles

STRETCH YOUR THINKING   E21

LESSON
5.3

Sum It Up

The shaded portion of each figure below models a fraction. Use the
figures to find each sum. Write your answer in simplest form.

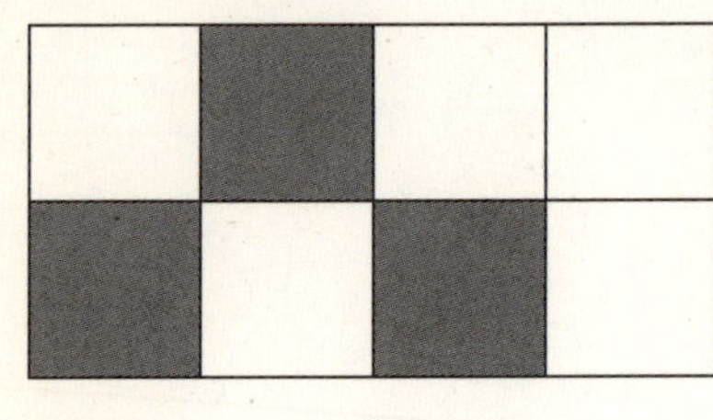

A

B

C

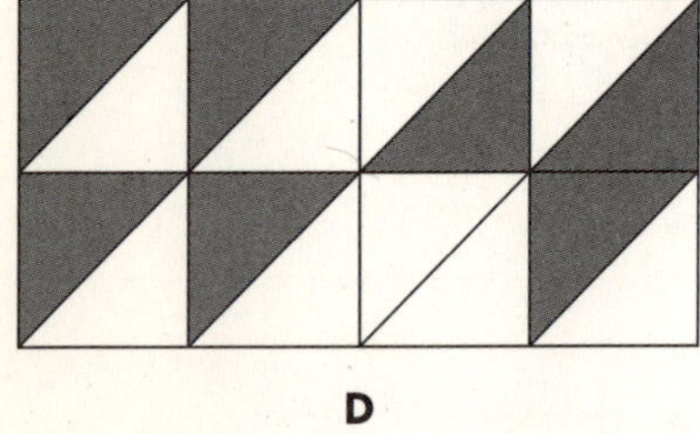

D

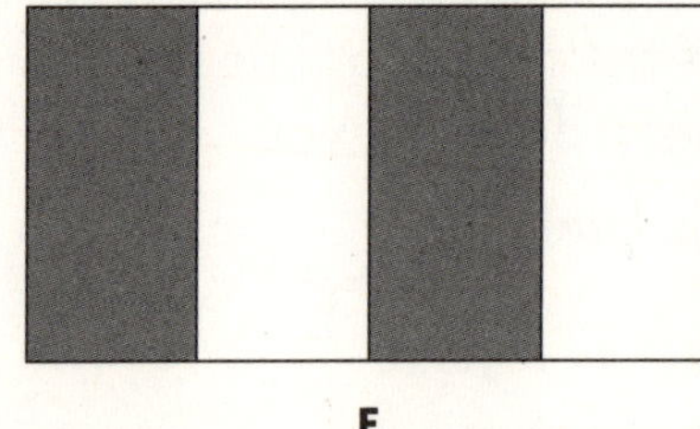

E

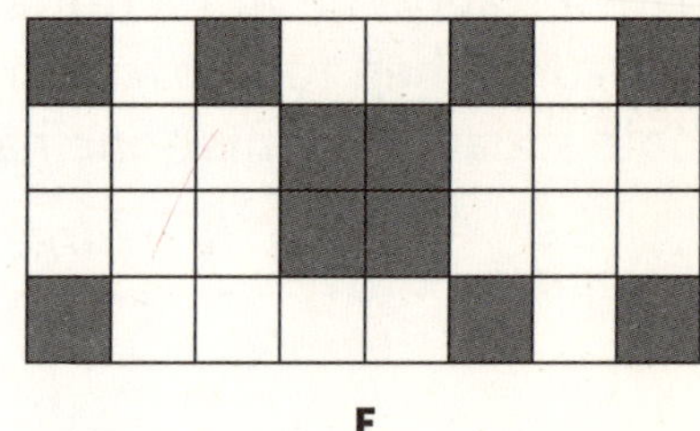

F

1. A + C = $\frac{5}{8}$

2. B + F = $\frac{21}{32}$

3. D + E = $\frac{15}{16}$

4. C + F = $\frac{19}{32}$

5. A + B = $\frac{11}{16}$

6. C + E = $\frac{3}{4}$

7. B + D = $\frac{3}{4}$

8. A + F = $\frac{23}{32}$

9. D + A = $\frac{13}{16}$

10. C + B = $\frac{9}{16}$

11. E + A = $\frac{7}{8}$

12. F + D = $\frac{25}{32}$

13. C + D = $\frac{11}{16}$

14. B + E + C = $1\frac{1}{16}$

15. F + A + D = $1\frac{5}{32}$

16. A + B + C = $\frac{15}{16}$

17. D + E + F = $1\frac{9}{32}$

18. A + F + B = $1\frac{1}{32}$

Think Like an Egyptian

Ancient Egyptians used only *unit fractions* to represent parts of a whole. (Unit fractions have 1 as the numerator.) This is how the ancient Egyptians wrote fractions by using symbols.

$$\text{☡} = \frac{1}{2} \qquad \text{☡} = \frac{1}{6} \qquad \text{☡} = \frac{1}{8}$$

$$\text{☡} = \frac{1}{11} \qquad \text{☡} = \frac{1}{12}$$

Look at the fractions above. Then use Egyptian symbols to represent these fractions.

1. $\frac{1}{4}$

2. $\frac{1}{10}$

3. $\frac{1}{5}$

4. $\frac{1}{7}$

Not every fraction has a 1 as a numerator. How did the Egyptians represent an amount like $\frac{3}{4}$? They showed it as a sum of two unit fractions.

$$\frac{1}{2} + \frac{1}{4} = \frac{3}{4}$$

Tell what fractions are being subtracted. Then find the difference. Write your answer using symbols as an ancient Egyptian would have.

5. $\frac{1}{2} - \frac{1}{3};$

6. $\frac{1}{4} - \frac{1}{8};$

7. $\frac{1}{3} - \frac{1}{4};$

8. $\frac{1}{4} - \frac{1}{5};$

9. $\frac{1}{2} - \frac{1}{5};$

10. $\frac{1}{4} - \frac{1}{10};$

STRETCH YOUR THINKING   E23

LESSON
5.5

You Pose the Problem

A mistake was made at the printer. This page should have contained eight word problems that require estimation of a sum or a difference of fractions. However, instead of the problems, the answers were printed.

Now you must create a word problem for each answer. Be sure that your problem requires estimating a sum or a difference. Exchange papers with a classmate. Check each other's work. **Check students' work.**

1. _______________________________

Answer: $\frac{1}{2}$ c flour

2. _______________________________

Answer: 1 yd fabric

3. _______________________________

Answer: 2 mi

4. _______________________________

Answer: 1 c sugar

5. _______________________________

Answer: $\frac{1}{2}$ in.

6. _______________________________

Answer: 1 mi

7. _______________________________

Answer: $\frac{1}{2}$ the flowers

8. _______________________________

Answer: 2 ft wire

Addition Patterns

Write the next three terms. Then identify the rule.

1. $10;\ 14\frac{1}{5};\ 18\frac{2}{5};\ 22\frac{3}{5};\ \underline{26\frac{4}{5}};\ \underline{31};\ \underline{35\frac{1}{5}}$

   Rule: Add $4\frac{1}{5}$ to previous term.

2. $1;\ 2\frac{1}{4};\ 3\frac{1}{2};\ 4\frac{3}{4};\ \underline{6};\ \underline{7\frac{1}{4}};\ \underline{8\frac{1}{2}}$

   Rule: Add $1\frac{1}{4}$ to previous term.

3. $5;\ 7\frac{1}{5};\ 9\frac{2}{5};\ 11\frac{3}{5};\ \underline{13\frac{4}{5}};\ \underline{16};\ \underline{18\frac{1}{5}}$

   Rule: Add $2\frac{1}{5}$ to previous term.

4. $1;\ 2\frac{3}{8};\ 3\frac{3}{4};\ 5\frac{1}{8};\ \underline{6\frac{1}{2}};\ \underline{7\frac{7}{8}};\ \underline{9\frac{1}{4}}$

   Rule: Add $1\frac{3}{8}$ to previous term.

5. $4;\ 7\frac{2}{9};\ 10\frac{4}{9};\ 13\frac{2}{3};\ \underline{16\frac{8}{9}};\ \underline{20\frac{1}{9}};\ \underline{23\frac{1}{3}}$

   Rule: Add $3\frac{2}{9}$ to previous term.

6. $2;\ 4\frac{3}{10};\ 6\frac{3}{5};\ 8\frac{9}{10};\ \underline{11\frac{1}{5}};\ \underline{13\frac{1}{2}};\ \underline{15\frac{4}{5}}$

   Rule: Add $2\frac{3}{10}$ to previous term.

7. $3;\ 4\frac{1}{3};\ 5\frac{2}{3};\ 7;\ \underline{8\frac{1}{3}};\ \underline{9\frac{2}{3}};\ \underline{11}$

   Rule: Add $1\frac{1}{3}$ to previous term.

8. $1;\ 3\frac{1}{6};\ 5\frac{1}{3};\ 7\frac{1}{2};\ \underline{9\frac{2}{3}};\ \underline{11\frac{5}{6}};\ \underline{14}$

   Rule: Add $2\frac{1}{6}$ to previous term.

9. $8;\ 9\frac{1}{8};\ 10\frac{1}{4};\ 11\frac{3}{8};\ \underline{12\frac{1}{2}};\ \underline{13\frac{5}{8}};\ \underline{14\frac{3}{4}}$

   Rule: Add $1\frac{1}{8}$ to previous term.

10. $2;\ 14\frac{3}{4};\ 17\frac{1}{2};\ 20\frac{1}{4};\ \underline{23};\ \underline{25\frac{3}{4}};\ \underline{28\frac{1}{2}}$

   Rule: Add $2\frac{3}{4}$ to previous term.

STRETCH YOUR THINKING   E25

Subtraction Patterns

Find the next three terms. Write the rule.

1. $19\frac{7}{8}$; $18\frac{5}{8}$; $17\frac{3}{8}$; $16\frac{1}{8}$; **$14\frac{7}{8}$** ; **$13\frac{5}{8}$** ; **$12\frac{3}{8}$**

   Rule: **Subtract $1\frac{2}{8}$ from previous term.**

2. 20; $18\frac{1}{2}$; 17; $15\frac{1}{2}$; **14** ; **$12\frac{1}{2}$** ; **11**

   Rule: **Subtract $1\frac{1}{2}$ from previous term.**

3. $24\frac{9}{10}$; $22\frac{6}{10}$; $20\frac{3}{10}$; 18; **$15\frac{7}{10}$** ; **$13\frac{2}{5}$** ; **$11\frac{1}{10}$**

   Rule: **Subtract $2\frac{3}{10}$ from previous term.**

4. $15\frac{7}{10}$; $14\frac{1}{2}$; $13\frac{3}{10}$; $12\frac{1}{10}$; **$10\frac{9}{10}$** ; **$9\frac{7}{10}$** ; **$8\frac{1}{2}$**

   Rule: **Subtract $1\frac{1}{5}$ from previous term.**

5. $14\frac{1}{2}$; $12\frac{3}{8}$; $10\frac{1}{4}$; $8\frac{1}{8}$; **6** ; **$3\frac{7}{8}$** ; **$1\frac{3}{4}$**

   Rule: **Subtract $2\frac{1}{8}$ from previous term.**

6. $9\frac{2}{3}$; $8\frac{5}{9}$; $7\frac{4}{9}$; $6\frac{1}{3}$; **$5\frac{2}{9}$** ; **$4\frac{1}{9}$** ; **3**

   Rule: **Subtract $1\frac{1}{9}$ from previous term.**

7. $18\frac{1}{2}$; $18\frac{1}{4}$; $17\frac{3}{4}$; 17; **16** ; **$14\frac{3}{4}$** ; **$13\frac{1}{4}$**

   Rule: **Subtract $\frac{1}{4}$, then $\frac{1}{2}$, then $\frac{3}{4}$, then 1, etc.**

8. 25; $24\frac{1}{4}$; $22\frac{1}{2}$; $19\frac{3}{4}$; **16** ; **$11\frac{1}{4}$** ; **$5\frac{1}{2}$**

   Rule: **Subtract $\frac{3}{4}$, then $1\frac{3}{4}$, then $2\frac{3}{4}$, then $3\frac{3}{4}$, etc.**

9. 39; $38\frac{1}{2}$; 37; $34\frac{1}{2}$; **31** ; **$26\frac{1}{2}$** ; **21**

   Rule: **Subtract $\frac{1}{2}$, then $1\frac{1}{2}$, then $2\frac{1}{2}$, then $3\frac{1}{2}$, etc.**

10. 42; $41\frac{7}{8}$; $40\frac{3}{4}$; $38\frac{5}{8}$; **$35\frac{1}{2}$** ; **$30\frac{3}{8}$** ; **$26\frac{1}{4}$**

    Rule: **Subtract $\frac{1}{8}$, then $1\frac{1}{8}$, then $2\frac{1}{8}$, then $3\frac{1}{8}$, etc.**

Puzzling Fractions

Match each Exercise in Column 1 with its sum or difference in
Column 2. Then, to discover the Math Tip in the box, write each
corresponding letter above the line marked with the Exercise number.

Column 1

1. $1\frac{1}{3} + 2\frac{3}{4}$ **H** ___

2. $5\frac{1}{2} - 3\frac{1}{4}$ **O** ___

3. $2\frac{2}{9} + 4\frac{8}{9}$ **A** ___

4. $6\frac{2}{3} - 5\frac{1}{3}$ **S** ___

5. $4\frac{5}{6} + 1\frac{2}{3}$ **D** ___

6. $5\frac{3}{10} - 1\frac{4}{5}$ **L** ___

7. $2\frac{1}{6} + 5\frac{1}{3}$ **U** ___

8. $6\frac{3}{4} - 3\frac{1}{6}$ **B** ___

9. $1\frac{1}{5} + 2\frac{1}{7}$ **N** ___

10. $7\frac{11}{12} - 5\frac{1}{6}$ **W** ___

11. $3\frac{3}{8} - 1\frac{1}{4}$ **E** ___

12. $6\frac{2}{5} + 1\frac{7}{20}$ **P** ___

13. $8\frac{5}{12} - 1\frac{5}{6}$ **I** ___

14. $5\frac{1}{3} + 1\frac{2}{7}$ **T** ___

15. $9\frac{2}{3} - 3\frac{2}{15}$ **M** ___

16. $4\frac{7}{10} - 2\frac{13}{20}$ **F** ___

17. $4\frac{2}{9} + 3\frac{1}{3}$ **R** ___

Column 2

A. $7\frac{1}{9}$

B. $3\frac{7}{12}$

D. $6\frac{1}{2}$

E. $2\frac{1}{8}$

F. $2\frac{1}{20}$

H. $4\frac{1}{12}$

I. $6\frac{7}{12}$

L. $3\frac{1}{2}$

M. $6\frac{8}{15}$

N. $3\frac{12}{35}$

O. $2\frac{1}{4}$

P. $7\frac{3}{4}$

R. $7\frac{5}{9}$

S. $1\frac{1}{3}$

T. $6\frac{13}{21}$

U. $7\frac{1}{2}$

W. $2\frac{3}{4}$

Math Tip

A	N	S	W	E	R	S		S	H	O	U	L	D
3	9	4	10	11	17	4		4	1	2	7	6	5

B	E		I	N
8	11		13	9

S	I	M	P	L	E	S	T		F	O	R	M	!
4	13	15	12	6	11	4	14		16	2	17	15	

STRETCH YOUR THINKING   E27

You Write the Problem

An error was made when this book was created. Somehow, the answers
to the problems on this page were printed, but the problems were
omitted. Help the printer out by creating an estimation problem for
each answer below. Make sure your problems involve mixed
numbers. **Problems will vary.**

1. ____

Answer – about $3\frac{1}{2}$ mi

2. ____

Answer – about 4 yd of fabric

3. ____

Answer – about 15 ft of wire

4. ____

Answer – about 3 c of flour

5. ____

Answer – about $7\frac{1}{2}$ yd of ribbon

6. ____

Answer – about 4 hr

7. ____

Answer – about 12 gal

8. ____

Answer – about $5\frac{1}{2}$ in.

Multiply to Find a Message

Match each exercise in Column 1 with its product in Column 2.
Then write each corresponding letter on the line below marked
with the exercise number to discover the Math Tip.

Column 1

1. $15 \times \frac{2}{5}$ ______ **H**
2. $\frac{5}{7} \times 14$ ______ **S**
3. $\frac{2}{3} \times \frac{1}{6}$ ______ **J**
4. $\frac{3}{8} \times \frac{4}{21}$ ______ **W**
5. $12 \times \frac{2}{3}$ ______ **A**
6. $\frac{1}{8} \times \frac{2}{7}$ ______ **O**
7. $13 \times \frac{1}{26}$ ______ **D**
8. $\frac{3}{10} \times \frac{5}{9}$ ______ **R**
9. $\frac{1}{4} \times \frac{20}{23}$ ______ **B**
10. $18 \times \frac{2}{3}$ ______ **L**
11. $\frac{7}{20} \times \frac{5}{14}$ ______ **T**
12. $\frac{1}{2} \times \frac{1}{5}$ ______ **Y**
13. $\frac{3}{12} \times \frac{2}{9}$ ______ **F**
14. $24 \times \frac{1}{6}$ ______ **U**
15. $\frac{6}{7} \times 21$ ______ **P**
16. $\frac{3}{10} \times 5$ ______ **I**
17. $\frac{9}{11} \times \frac{1}{3}$ ______ **C**
18. $\frac{13}{25} \times \frac{5}{6}$ ______ **Q**
19. $\frac{4}{5} \times 35$ ______ **E**
20. $\frac{9}{10} \times \frac{2}{3}$ ______ **V**
21. $\frac{1}{10} \times 9$ ______ **K**
22. $\frac{3}{7} \times 35$ ______ **M**
23. $\frac{5}{9} \times \frac{18}{25}$ ______ **N**
24. $\frac{1}{3} \times 5$ ______ **Z**
25. $\frac{7}{10} \times 3$ ______ **G**
26. $\frac{1}{2} \times \frac{6}{7}$ ______ **X**

Column 2

A. 8	N. $\frac{2}{5}$
B. $\frac{5}{23}$	O. $\frac{1}{28}$
C. $\frac{3}{11}$	P. 18
D. $\frac{1}{2}$	Q. $\frac{13}{30}$
E. 28	R. $\frac{1}{6}$
F. $\frac{1}{18}$	S. 10
G. $2\frac{1}{10}$	T. $\frac{1}{8}$
H. 6	U. 4
I. $1\frac{1}{2}$	V. $\frac{3}{5}$
J. $\frac{1}{9}$	W. $\frac{1}{14}$
K. $\frac{9}{10}$	X. $\frac{3}{7}$
L. 12	Y. $\frac{1}{10}$
M. 15	Z. $1\frac{2}{3}$

M A __ F R A C T I O N
   5   13   8   5   17   11   16   6   23

A

T G R E A T E R __ T H A N
  25   8   19   5   11   19   8   11   1   5   23

H O N E __ C A N __ B E
  6   23   19   17   5   23   9   19

T

I W R I T T E N __ A S __ A
  4   8   16   11   11   19   23   5   2   5

P M I X E D __ N U M B E R.
  22   16   26   19   7   23   14   22   9   19   8

STRETCH YOUR THINKING   E29

Fraction Flowers

Color the petals containing factors of the product in the circle. Remember to use GCFs to simplify the factors before multiplying!

1.

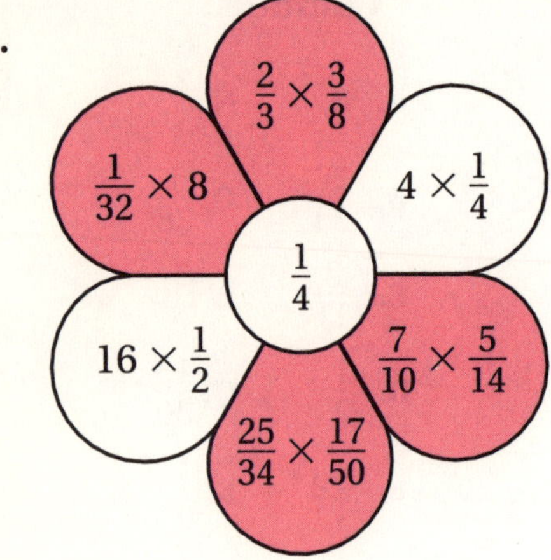

2.

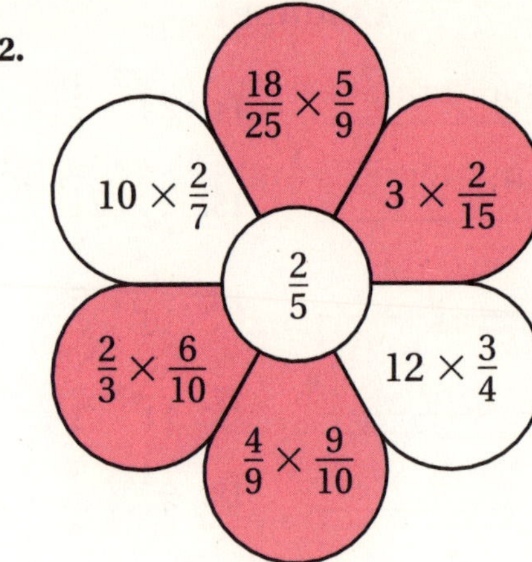

3.

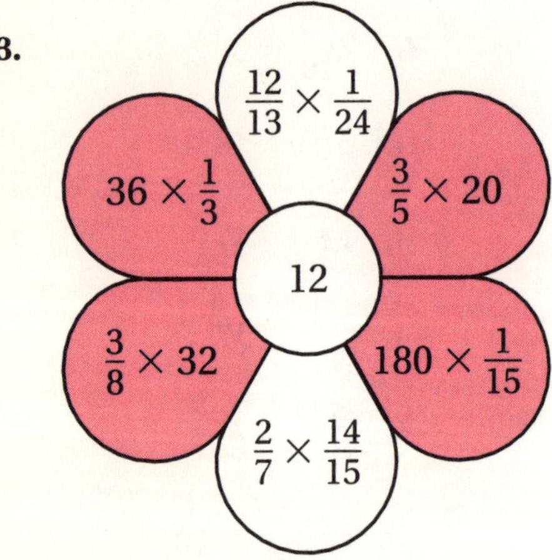

4.

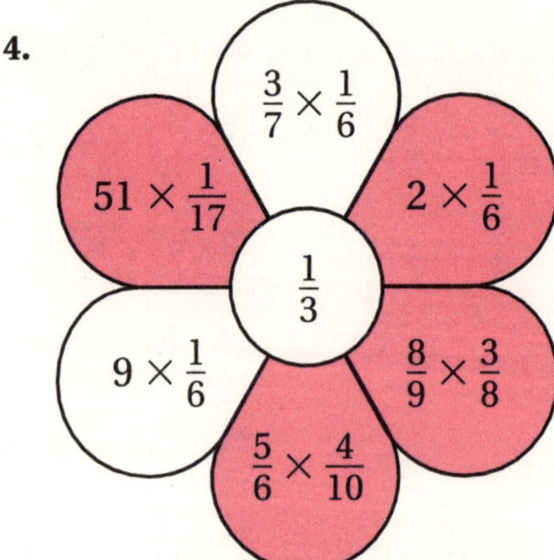

5.

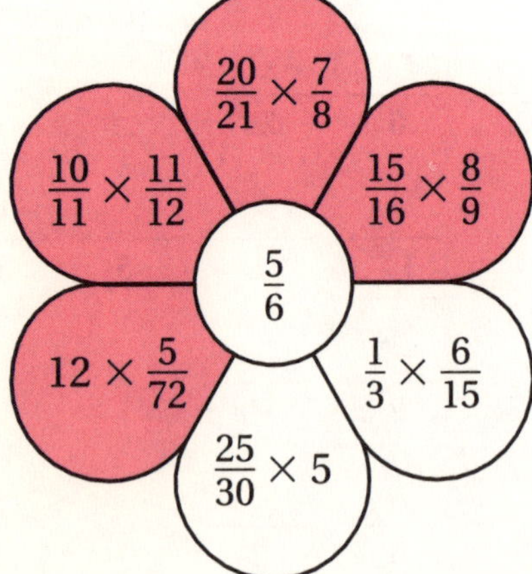

6.

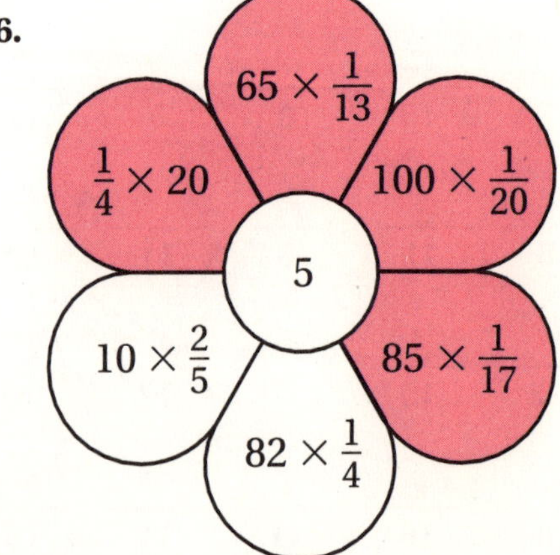

Fraction Analogies

Read each analogy. Explain how each pair of numbers are related.
The first one is done for you.

1. $2\frac{1}{3}$ is to $3\frac{1}{2}$ as $4\frac{3}{8}$ is to $6\frac{9}{16}$.

   Think: What number times $2\frac{1}{3}$ equals $3\frac{1}{2}$.

   $3\frac{1}{2}$ is the product of $2\frac{1}{3}$ and $1\frac{1}{2}$, just as $6\frac{9}{16}$ is the product of $4\frac{3}{8}$ and $1\frac{1}{2}$.

2. $1\frac{2}{5}$ is to $2\frac{9}{20}$ as $3\frac{1}{2}$ is to $6\frac{1}{8}$.

   $2\frac{9}{20}$ is the product of $1\frac{2}{5}$ and $1\frac{3}{4}$, as $6\frac{1}{8}$ is the product of $3\frac{1}{2}$ and $1\frac{3}{4}$.

3. $4\frac{3}{8}$ is to $1\frac{3}{32}$ as $5\frac{3}{4}$ is to $1\frac{7}{16}$.

   $1\frac{3}{32}$ is the product of $4\frac{3}{8}$ and $\frac{1}{4}$, as $1\frac{7}{16}$ is the product of $5\frac{3}{4}$ and $\frac{1}{4}$.

4. $3\frac{4}{5}$ is to $9\frac{1}{2}$ as $4\frac{7}{8}$ is to $12\frac{3}{16}$.

   $9\frac{1}{2}$ is the product of $3\frac{4}{5}$ and $2\frac{1}{2}$, as $12\frac{3}{16}$ is the product of $4\frac{7}{8}$ and $2\frac{1}{2}$.

5. $5\frac{1}{3}$ is to $1\frac{1}{15}$ as $6\frac{3}{4}$ is to $1\frac{7}{20}$.

   $1\frac{1}{15}$ is the product of $5\frac{1}{3}$ and $\frac{1}{5}$, as $1\frac{7}{20}$ is the product of $6\frac{3}{4}$ and $\frac{1}{5}$.

6. $9\frac{5}{6}$ is to $11\frac{1}{16}$ as $3\frac{1}{4}$ is to $3\frac{21}{32}$.

   $11\frac{1}{16}$ is the product of $9\frac{5}{6}$ and $1\frac{1}{8}$, as $3\frac{21}{32}$ is the product of $3\frac{1}{4}$ and $1\frac{1}{8}$.

7. $2\frac{5}{12}$ is to $3\frac{2}{9}$ as $4\frac{5}{6}$ is to $6\frac{4}{9}$.

   $3\frac{2}{9}$ is the product of $2\frac{5}{12}$ and $1\frac{1}{3}$, as $6\frac{4}{9}$ is the product of $4\frac{5}{6}$ and $1\frac{1}{3}$.

STRETCH YOUR THINKING **E31**

Divide to Find a Message

Match each exercise in Column 1 with its quotient in Column 2.
Then write each corresponding letter on the line below marked
with the exercise number to discover the Math Tip.

Column 1

1. $\frac{3}{4} \div \frac{1}{2}$ _____ **L**
2. $6 \div \frac{1}{9}$ _____ **Q**
3. $\frac{8}{11} \div \frac{1}{3}$ _____ **G**
4. $10 \div \frac{2}{5}$ _____ **A**
5. $\frac{11}{12} \div \frac{1}{3}$ _____ **N**
6. $\frac{1}{10} \div 5$ _____ **C**
7. $\frac{3}{4} \div \frac{1}{8}$ _____ **T**
8. $\frac{5}{7} \div 10$ _____ **X**
9. $\frac{4}{5} \div \frac{2}{10}$ _____ **Z**
10. $3 \div \frac{2}{9}$ _____ **E**
11. $8 \div \frac{3}{8}$ _____ **V**
12. $\frac{7}{8} \div \frac{1}{2}$ _____ **B**
13. $\frac{1}{2} \div 2$ _____ **S**

14. $12 \div \frac{1}{6}$ _____ **U**
15. $\frac{2}{7} \div \frac{1}{8}$ _____ **P**
16. $18 \div \frac{2}{3}$ _____ **J**
17. $\frac{3}{20} \div \frac{3}{10}$ _____ **I**
18. $15 \div \frac{1}{3}$ _____ **W**
19. $\frac{3}{5} \div \frac{1}{3}$ _____ **R**
20. $11 \div \frac{1}{2}$ _____ **D**
21. $\frac{5}{7} \div \frac{10}{14}$ _____ **F**
22. $\frac{2}{3} \div \frac{8}{9}$ _____ **Y**
23. $5 \div \frac{1}{15}$ _____ **H**
24. $\frac{7}{8} \div \frac{1}{4}$ _____ **O**
25. $10 \div \frac{1}{5}$ _____ **K**
26. $\frac{5}{8} \div \frac{1}{3}$ _____ **M**

Column 2

A. 25
B. $1\frac{3}{4}$
C. $\frac{1}{50}$
D. 22
E. $13\frac{1}{2}$
F. 1
G. $2\frac{2}{11}$
H. 75
I. $\frac{1}{2}$
J. 27
K. 50
L. $1\frac{1}{2}$
M. $1\frac{7}{8}$
N. $2\frac{3}{4}$
O. $3\frac{1}{2}$
P. $2\frac{2}{7}$
Q. 54
R. $1\frac{4}{5}$
S. $\frac{1}{4}$
T. 6
U. 72
V. $21\frac{1}{3}$
W. 45
X. $\frac{1}{14}$
Y. $\frac{3}{4}$
Z. 4

M
T (7) H (23) E (10)   P (15) R (19) O (24) D (20) U (14) C (6) T (7)

A

T
O (24) F (21)   A (4)   N (5) U (14) M (26) B (12) E (10) R (19)

H
A (4) N (5) D (20)   I (17) T (7) S (13)

T

I
R (19) E (10) C (6) I (17) P (15) R (19) O (24) C (6) A (4) L (1)

P
I (17) S (13)   O (24) N (5) E (10).

Secret Letter

Solve each problem by working backward. Find a box below with the
same number. Shade the box to find the secret letter.

1. The area of a rectangular garden is
$34\frac{5}{6}$ sq ft. The length is $6\frac{1}{3}$ ft. What is
the width of the garden?

$5\frac{1}{2}$ ft

2. Rick chose a number and multiplied
it by $2\frac{1}{4}$. The product was 18. What
was the number?

8

3. Bill has 10 yd of plastic. This is 6 times
the amount he needs to cover a table.
How much plastic does he need to
cover one table?

$1\frac{2}{3}$ yd

4. Joan has a 5-lb bag of potatoes. She
uses $2\frac{1}{2}$ lb for a recipe. How many
times can she make the recipe from
that bag?

2 times

5. Rachel bought a rectangular rug for
her living room. The area of the rug is
133 sq ft. The length of the rug is 14 ft.
What is the width of the rug?

$9\frac{1}{2}$ ft

6. Joel has a $3\frac{1}{2}$-lb box of detergent. He
uses $\frac{1}{4}$ lb to wash his car. How many
car washings will he get from his
supply?

14 washings

14	2	8
$2\frac{1}{5}$	$9\frac{1}{2}$	$3\frac{1}{3}$
$4\frac{2}{3}$	$5\frac{1}{2}$	40
$6\frac{5}{8}$	$1\frac{2}{3}$	$2\frac{1}{2}$

The secret letter is ______T______ .

STRETCH YOUR THINKING **E33**

Let Me Count the Ways

1. Name the line in 12 different ways.

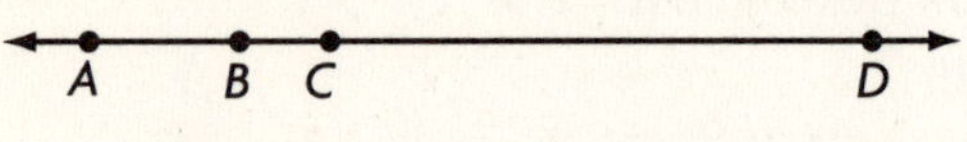

$$\overleftrightarrow{AB}, \overleftrightarrow{BA}, \overleftrightarrow{BC}, \overleftrightarrow{CB}, \overleftrightarrow{CD}, \overleftrightarrow{DC}, \overleftrightarrow{AC}, \overleftrightarrow{CA}, \overleftrightarrow{BD}, \overleftrightarrow{DB}, \overleftrightarrow{AD}, \overleftrightarrow{DA}$$

2. There are 12 different line segments in the figure. Name them.

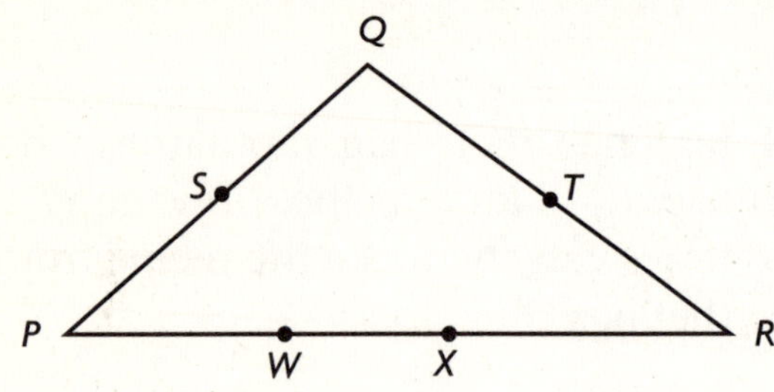

$$\overline{PQ}, \overline{PS}, \overline{SQ}, \overline{QT}, \overline{TR}, \overline{QR}, \overline{PW}, \overline{WX}, \overline{XR}, \overline{PX}, \overline{WR}, \overline{PR}$$

3. Name six different rays in the figure.

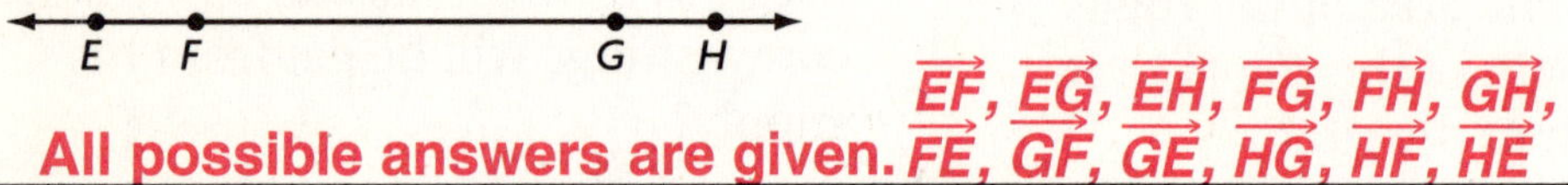

All possible answers are given. $\overrightarrow{EF}, \overrightarrow{EG}, \overrightarrow{EH}, \overrightarrow{FG}, \overrightarrow{FH}, \overrightarrow{GH},$ $\overrightarrow{FE}, \overrightarrow{GF}, \overrightarrow{GE}, \overrightarrow{HG}, \overrightarrow{HF}, \overrightarrow{HE}$

4. Name the plane in 10 different ways, using three points each time.

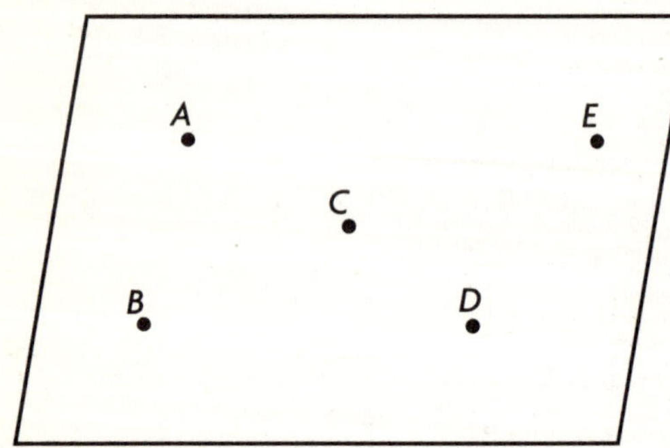

ABC, ABD, ABE, BCD, BCE, ACD, ACE, ADE, BDE, CDE

5. On a ruler, suppose you mark a point at each inch, half inch, quarter inch, and eighth inch. The ruler is 12 inches long. How many points are marked?

96 points

Space Project

In a plane, two lines are either parallel or intersecting. But *in space*, there are three possibilities: parallel, intersecting, and *skew* (SKYOO).

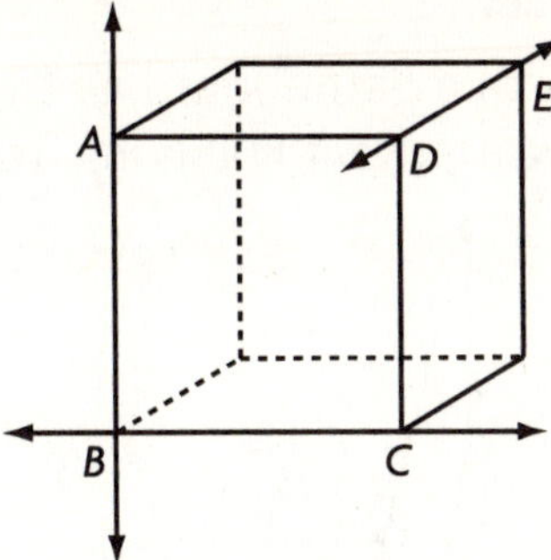

Look at the lines that form the edges of the cube. $\overleftrightarrow{AB}$ and $\overleftrightarrow{DE}$ are skew lines. They don't intersect, and they are not parallel. Also, $\overleftrightarrow{BC}$ and $\overleftrightarrow{DE}$ are skew lines.

Look at your classroom.

- There is a line where the front wall meets the ceiling. Call it line 1.
- There is a line where the front wall meets the floor. Call it line 2.
- There is a line where the right side wall meets the ceiling. Call it line 3.

Are the lines parallel, intersecting, or skew?

1. lines 1 and 2

 parallel

2. lines 2 and 3

 skew

3. lines 1 and 3

 intersecting

For Exercises 4–10, use the figure at the right.
Tell whether the lines are parallel, intersecting, or skew.

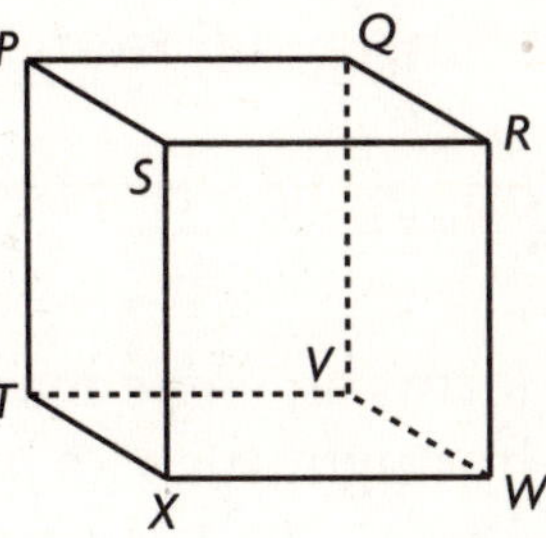

4. $\overleftrightarrow{SR}$ and $\overleftrightarrow{TX}$ **skew**

5. $\overleftrightarrow{VW}$ and $\overleftrightarrow{QR}$ **parallel**

6. $\overleftrightarrow{SP}$ and $\overleftrightarrow{QP}$ **intersecting**

7. $\overleftrightarrow{PT}$ and $\overleftrightarrow{XW}$ **skew**

8. $\overleftrightarrow{TV}$ and $\overleftrightarrow{RW}$ **skew**

9. $\overleftrightarrow{TV}$ and $\overleftrightarrow{SR}$ **parallel**

10. $\overleftrightarrow{PS}$ and $\overleftrightarrow{QV}$ **skew**

STRETCH YOUR THINKING   E35

Angles in 3-D

An angle is formed by two rays or lines that lie in a plane. You can also talk about the angle formed when two planes intersect. This angle can be acute, right, or obtuse.

Think of the two halves of a gameboard as two intersecting planes. As you unfold the gameboard, the angle goes from acute, to right, to obtuse.

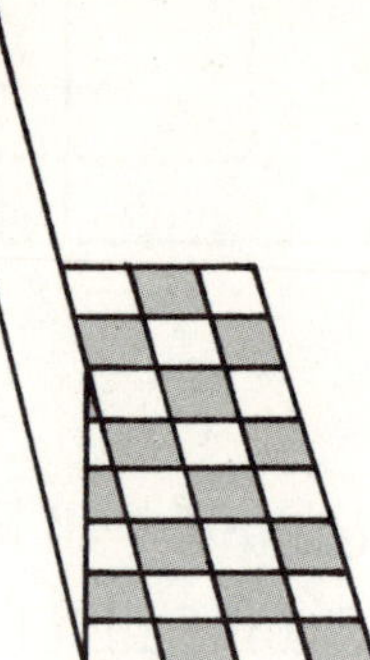
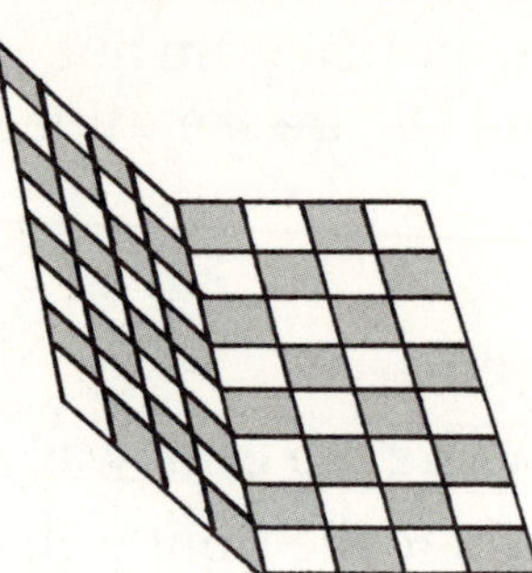

Answer these questions about real-life situations that involve angles formed by intersecting planes.

1. When you play chess, the gameboard is unfolded to what type of angle?

   straight

2. What does it mean when a door is "ajar"? What kind of angle is formed between the door and the wall?

   It is open just a little; acute.

3. An adjustable outdoor lounge chair has several settings. What types of angles can be formed by the seat and back of the chair?

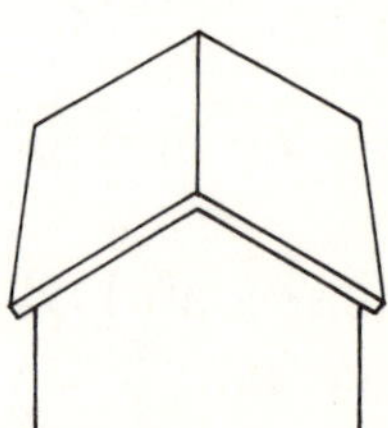

   The settings will result in obtuse angles and possibly a right or straight angle.

4. A roof line forms an angle made by the two sides of the roof. Why might such an angle be acute? obtuse? Discuss.

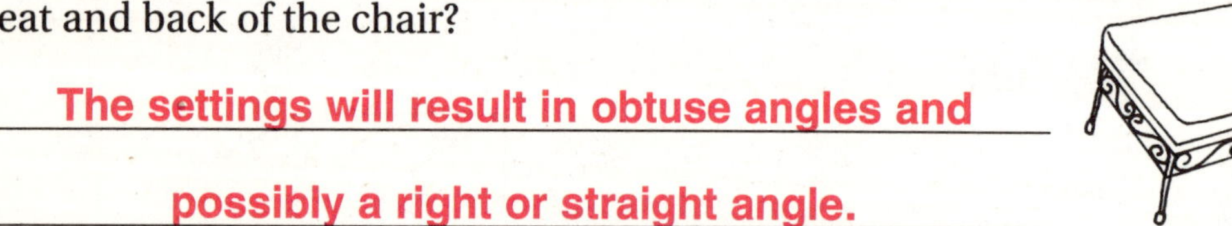

   The angle can vary simply for the sake of appearance, or the variations may serve a function.

   A steep roof, forming an acute angle, might be appropriate in areas where heavy snow falls.

Measure Up

Use a ruler and a protractor to measure the sides and angles of each figure.
List all pairs of congruent sides or angles for each figure.

1.

$\overline{AD} \cong \overline{BC}, \angle A \cong \angle B, \angle D \cong \angle C$

2.

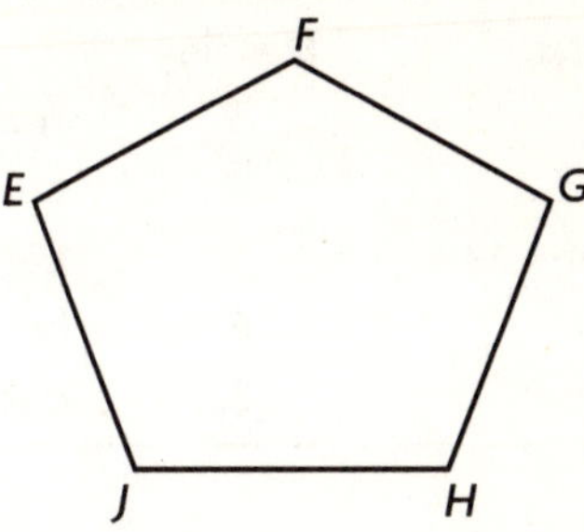

$\overline{EJ} \cong \overline{GH}, \overline{EF} \cong \overline{GF}, \angle J \cong \angle H,$

$\angle E \cong \angle G$

3.

$\overline{KN} \cong \overline{LM}, \overline{KL} \cong \overline{NM}, \angle N \cong \angle L,$

$\angle K \cong \angle M$

4.

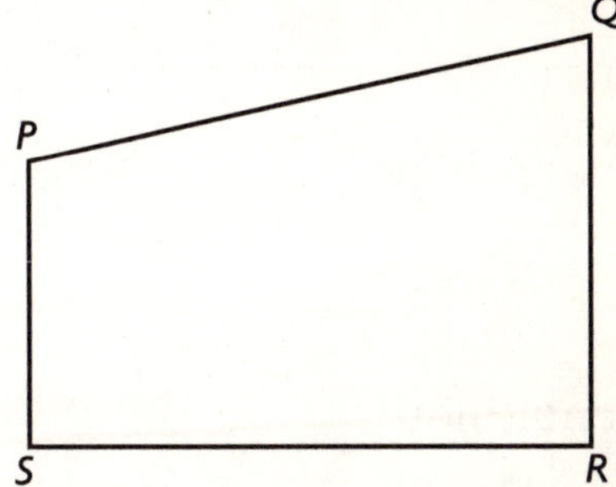

$\overline{SR} \cong \overline{RQ}, \angle S \cong \angle R$

5.

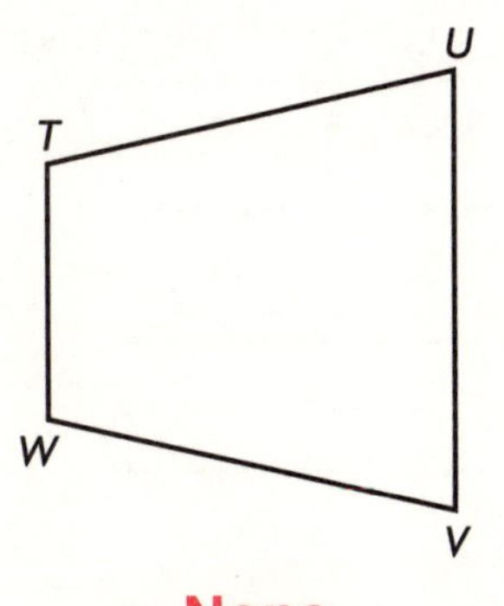

None

6.

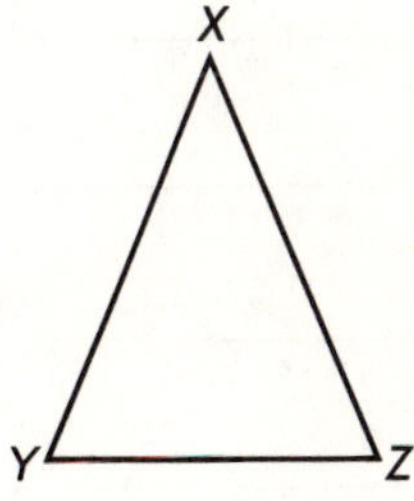

$\overline{XY} \cong \overline{XZ}, \angle Y \cong \angle Z$

Look It Up!

Tri-, *quad-*, and so on are prefixes. Study the table.

Prefix	Meaning	Polygon
tri-	3	triangle (3 sides)
quad-	4	quadrilateral (4 sides)
pent-	5	pentagon (5 sides)
hex-	6	hexagon (6 sides)
oct-	8	octagon (8 sides)

There are many other words that use these prefixes. Define each of these words. First try defining them without a dictionary. Then use a dictionary to check your definitions.

1. tricycle _______ a three-wheeled vehicle _______

2. quadruplets _______ four offspring born at one birth _______

3. pentathlon _______ an athletic contest involving five _______ different events

4. octave _______ a stanza of eight lines or an eight-day _______ period of holiday observances

5. quadruped _______ an animal having four feet _______

6. tripod _______ a three-legged stand _______

7. octet _______ a musical composition for eight _______ instruments or voices

8. hexameter _______ a line of verse consisting of six _______ metrical feet

Symmetry Puzzler

These eight figures are all congruent. They have the same size and
shape. Only their positions are different. They contain no line or
rotational symmetry, but they can be copied and combined to create
symmetric figures.

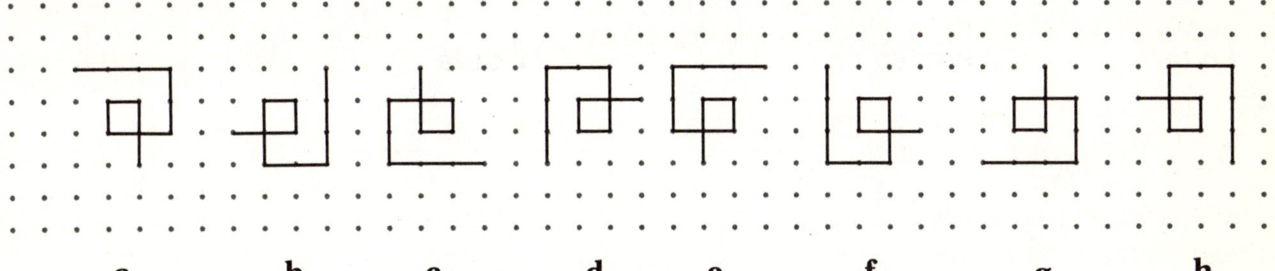

a.   b.   c.   d.   e.   f.   g.   h.

Identify which of the figures have been combined, without overlapping,
to create each design.

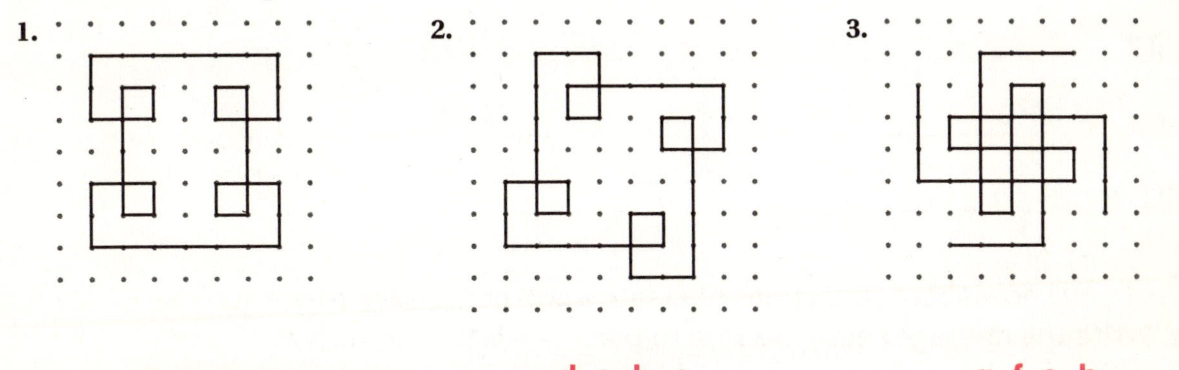

1. __________ e, a, g, c __________

2. __________ d, a, b, c __________

3. __________ g, f, e, h __________

Use the figures to create two different symmetric designs of your own.
Be sure each one is made from congruent parts in different positions.
Check students' drawings.

Mirror Images

When you look in a mirror, you see a reflection of your image. Look
at the letters below. Predict the words they will become if held to
a mirror. Write your predictions on the lines. Then, hold the paper
against a mirror and check your predictions. **Students' predictions
may vary.**

Letters	Predictions	Words
1. MOM	__________	**MOM**
2. WOT	__________	**TOW**
3. XIM	__________	**MIX**
4. TIH	__________	**HIT**
5. TAH	__________	**HAT**
6. XAM	__________	**MAX**
7. MIT	__________	**TIM**

Use what you know about reflections to create a secret message to a
friend. Write the message below. Be sure to place the letters in such a
way that they can be read when reflected in a mirror!
Check students' messages.

Gift Wrap Design

Pretend you work for a greeting card company. You have been asked to
create a new design for gift wrap. Your design must be a tessellation
that uses three different colors. Sketch your design in the cube below.
Then use crayons or markers to show its colors.

Check students' designs.

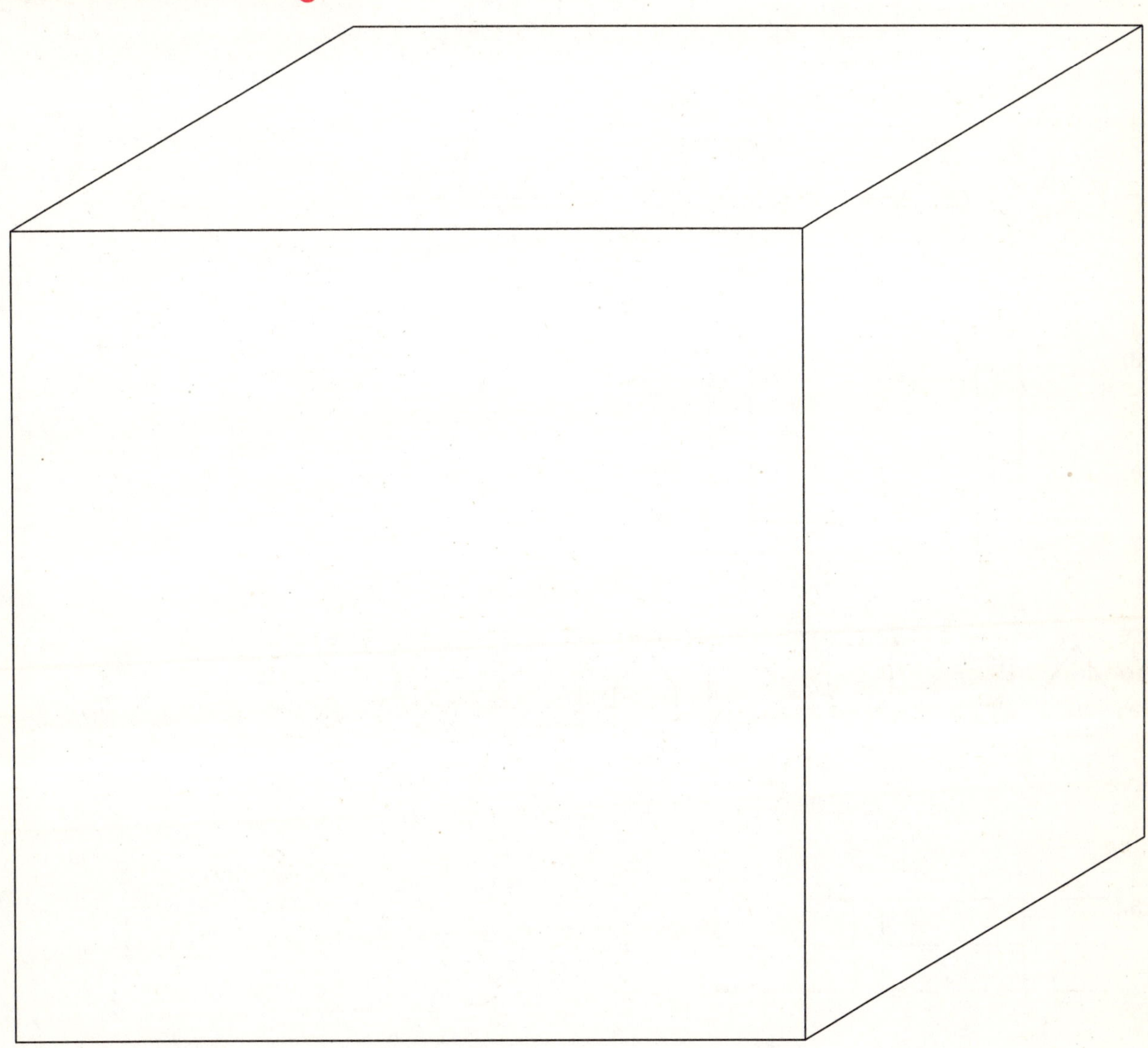

Puzzling Patterns

Draw the next two figures in each pattern.

1.

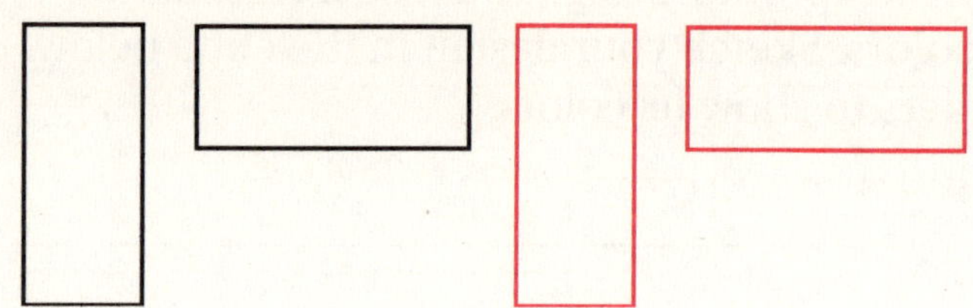

2.

3.

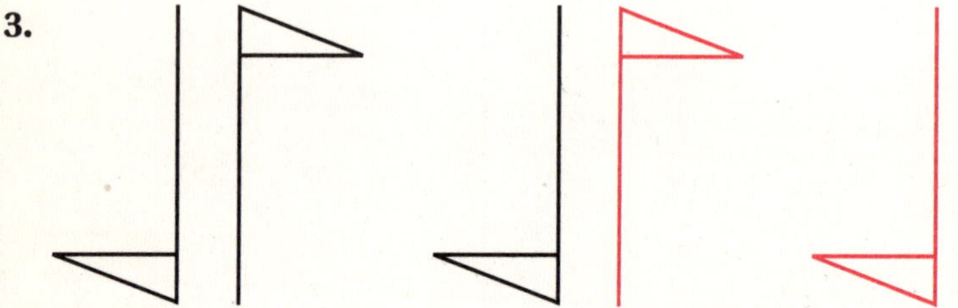

4.

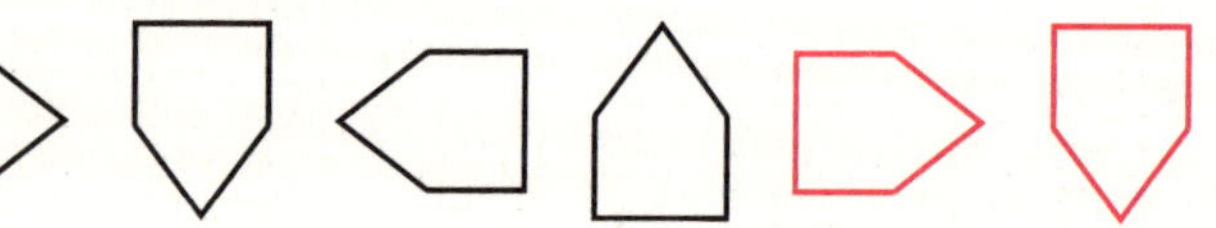

5.

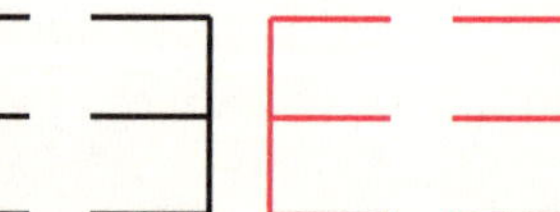

6.

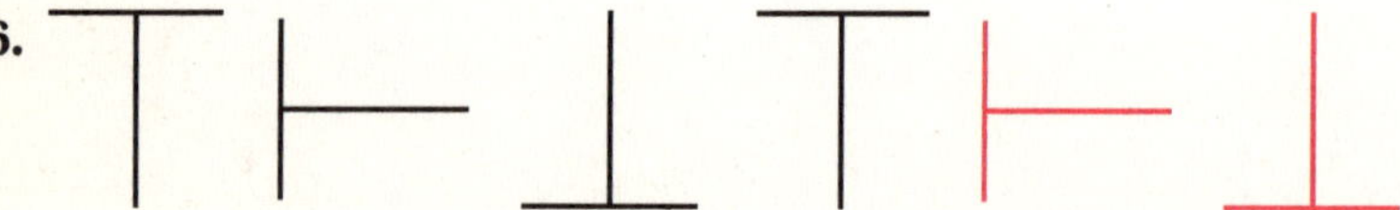

Cross-Figure Puzzle

Use the names of the figures below to complete the puzzle.

Across

1. 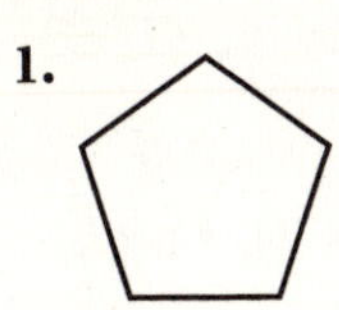

2.

3.

4.

5.

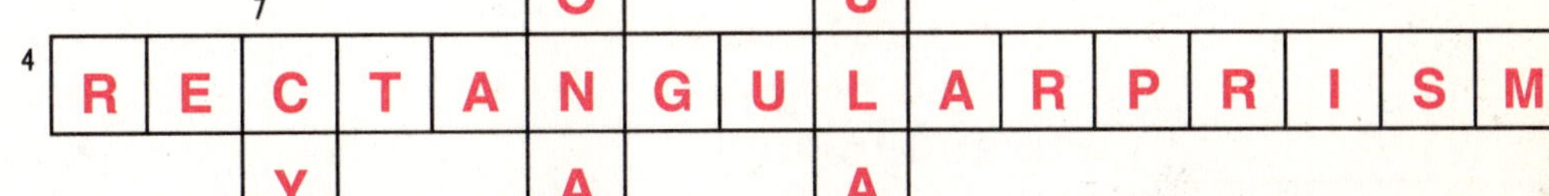
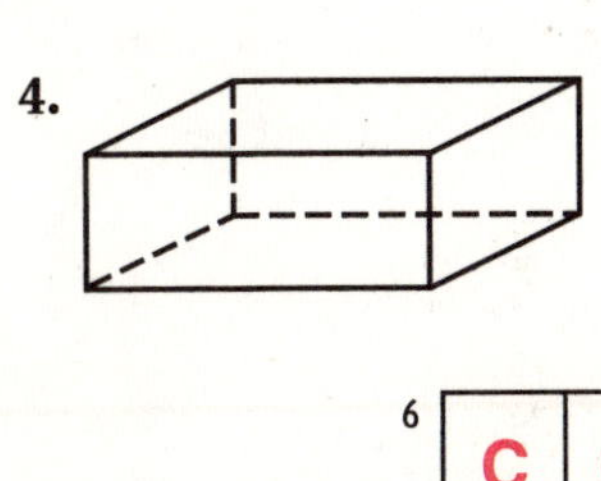
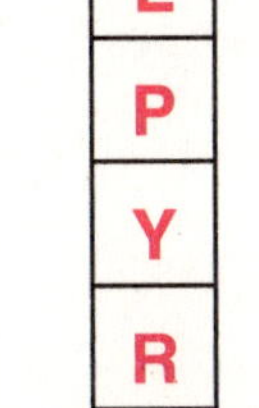
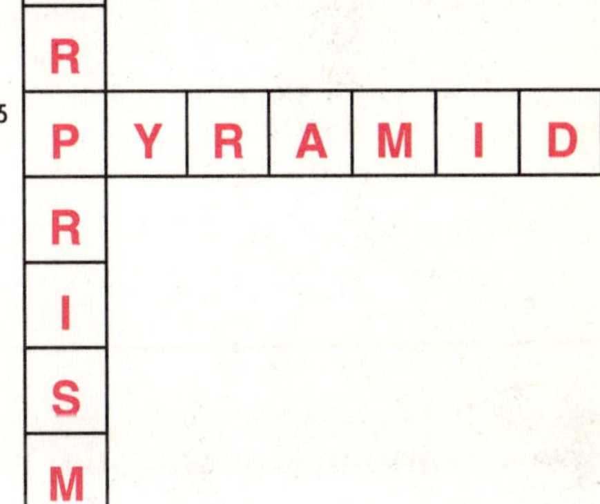

Down

6. 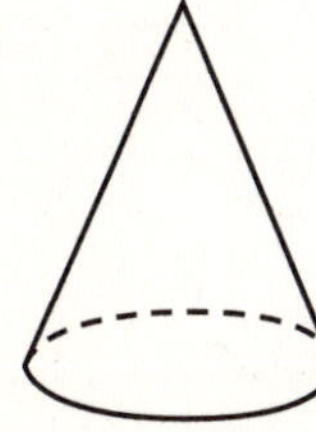   1. 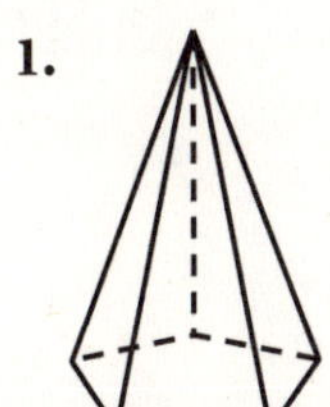   7. 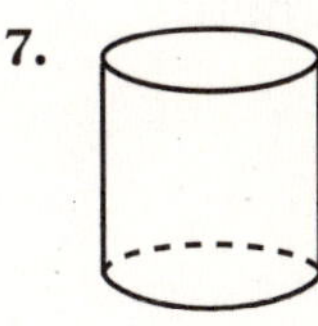   8. 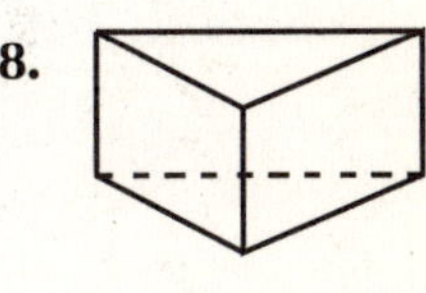

9. How are the figures shown for 6 Across and 7 Down similar? How are they different?

Both have a circular base and a curved lateral surface;

a cone has 1 base and a vertex.

STRETCH YOUR THINKING   E43

Ornament Creations

A group of students combined solid figures to create unusual ornaments. Read about each student's creation. Then answer the questions that follow.

1. For her ornament, Ricki glued together 2 rectangular prisms. Her creation has 6 faces and 8 vertices.

- How many edges does her creation have?

12 edges

- Sketch Ricki's ornament.

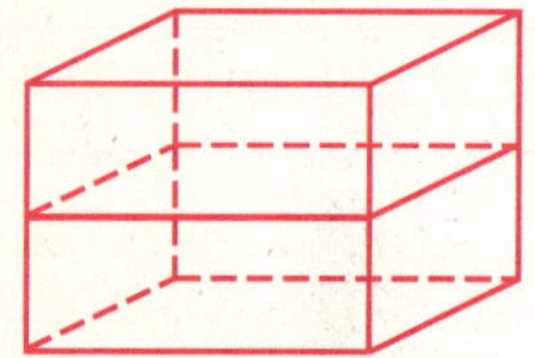

Prisms could also be glued end-to-end.

2. Seth glued together 2 rectangular pyramids. His creation has 10 faces and 16 edges.

- How many vertices does Seth's ornament have?

8 vertices

- Sketch Seth's ornament.

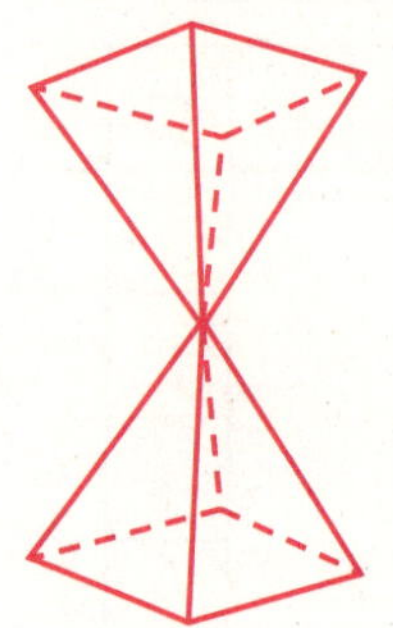

Pyramids could also be glued base-to-base.

3. Tonya combined a triangular prism and a triangular pyramid. Her creation has 7 faces and 12 edges.

- How many vertices does Tonya's creation have?

7 vertices

- Sketch Tonya's ornament.

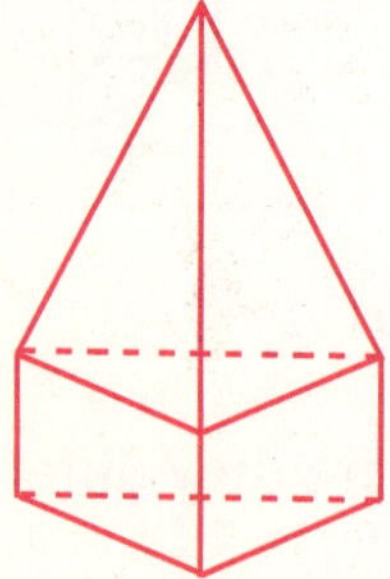

4. Rusty combined a pentagonal prism and a pentagonal pyramid. His creation has 11 faces and 11 vertices.

- How many edges does his ornament have?

20 edges

- Sketch Rusty's ornament.

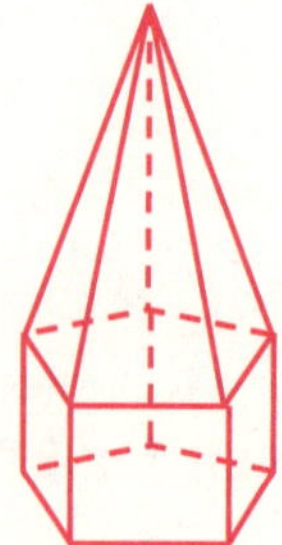

X Marks the Spot

Is the arrangement a net for a cube? Write *yes* or *no*. If *yes*, then write
the letter that will be opposite the X.

1.

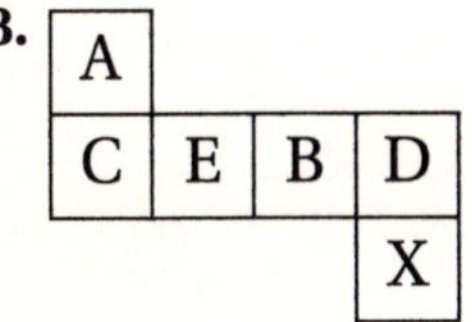

___________ **yes; E**

2.

C X A
E B D

___________ **no**

3.

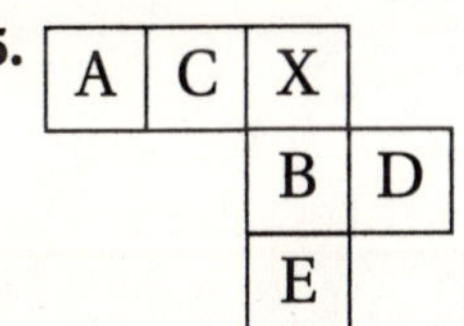

___________ **yes; A**

4.

A X C
   B D E

___________ **yes; D**

5.

A C X
   B D
  E

___________ **no**

6.

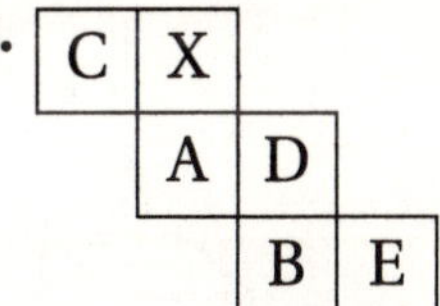

___________ **yes; B**

7.

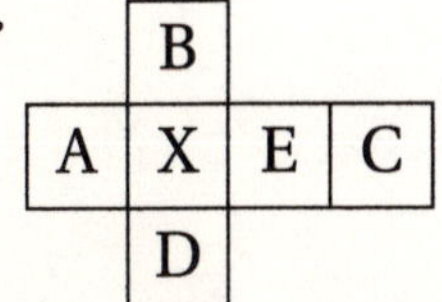

___________ **yes; C**

8.

B C D E
X   A

___________ **no**

STRETCH YOUR THINKING   E45

What's Your View?

If you fold the net below into a cube, which cubes below are different views of the cube? Write *yes* or *no*.

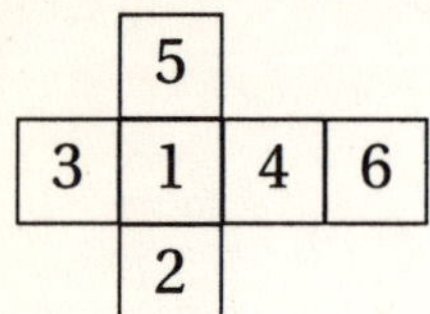

1. 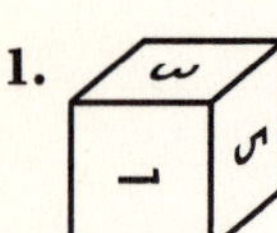

yes

2. 

yes

3. 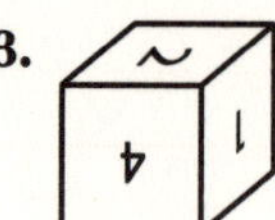

yes

4. 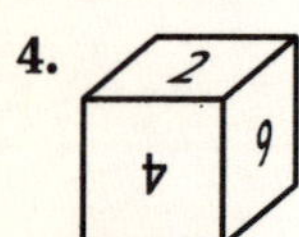

no

5. 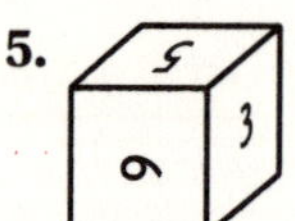

no

6. 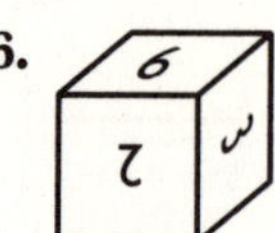

yes

7. 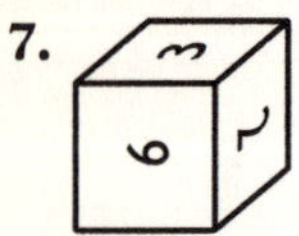

yes

8. 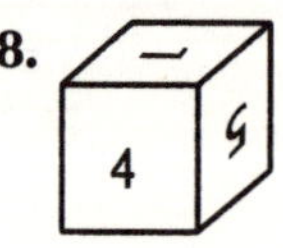

no

9. 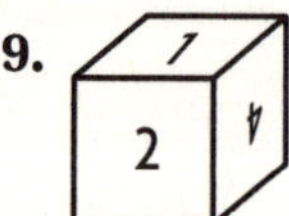

no

10. 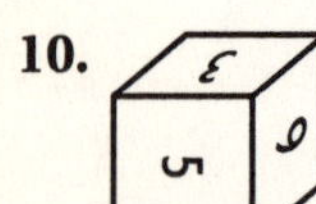

yes

11. 

no

12. 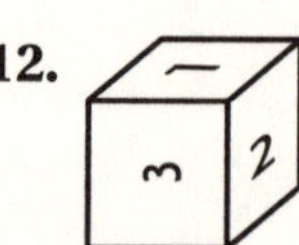

yes

Number Patterns

Name the next three terms. Then identify the rule used to form the
pattern.

1. 28, 32, 40, 52, __68__, __88__, __112__

   Rule: ____Add 4, then 8, then 12, then 16, and so on.____

2. 132, 127, 117, 102, __82__, __57__, __27__

   Rule: ____Subtract 5, then 10, then 15, then 20, and so on.____

3. 43, 55, 77, 109, __151__, __203__, __265__

   Rule: ____Add 12, then 22, then 32, then 42, and so on.____

4. 154, 147, 133, 112, __84__, __49__, __7__

   Rule: ____Subtract 7, then 14, then 21, then 28, and so on.____

5. 63, 72, 90, 126, __198__, __342__, __630__

   Rule: ____Add 9, then 18, then 36, then 72, and so on.____

6. 117, 109, 125, 117, 133, __125__, __141__, __133__

   Rule: ____Subtract 8, then add 16.____

7. 203, 181, 161, 143, __127__, __113__, __101__

   Rule: ____Subtract 22, then 20, then 18, then 16, and so on.____

8. 97, 112, 129, 148, __169__, __192__, __217__

   Rule: ____Add 15, then 17, then 19, then 21, and so on.____

9. 101, 121, 140, 158, __175__, __191__, __206__

   Rule: ____Add 20, then 19, then 18, then 17, and so on.____

10. 200, 175, 152, 131, __112__, __95__, __80__

    Rule: ____Subtract 25, then 23, then 21, then 19, and so on.____

It's Logical

Read about each situation. Write *T* for a true statement or *F* for a false statement.

1. Jon exercises every day. On weekends, he jogs. During the week, he alternately rides a bicycle or swims.

   __F__ If Jon swims today, then tomorrow he will definitely ride a bicycle.

   __F__ Jon never exercises the same way for two days in a row.

   __T__ If Jon is jogging, then it must be Saturday or Sunday.

2. Ruth and Bev are sisters. They take turns cooking meals. On each odd-numbered date, Ruth makes breakfast and Bev makes dinner. The sisters switch jobs on even-numbered dates.

   __F__ Ruth makes dinner on July 5.

   __T__ Each sister makes only one meal a day.

   __T__ During the month of May, Bev prepares more dinners than Ruth.

3. A baseball team is lined up for batting practice. The pitcher is standing behind the first baseman. The shortstop is standing in front of the catcher. The second baseman is standing between the catcher and the first baseman. The pitcher is last in line.

   __T__ The shortstop is first in line.

   __T__ The first baseman is standing behind the second baseman.

   __F__ The catcher is standing behind the pitcher.

4. The zigot factory produces zigots every day of the week. Each weekday, the factory makes 15,000 zigots. The total number of zigots made on weekends is equal to that made in one weekday. The same number of zigots are made on Saturday and Sunday.

   __F__ The factory makes 105,000 zigots each week.

   __F__ On Saturday, the factory makes $\frac{1}{7}$ of its weekly total.

   __T__ The number of zigots made on Sunday is half the amount made on Monday.

5. Sal and Anne drove 400 miles to visit a relative. Sal drove the first 140 miles. Anne then drove $1\frac{1}{2}$ times that distance. Sal drove the remaining distance.

   __F__ Sal drove more miles than Anne.

   __T__ Anne drove more than half the total distance.

   __T__ To have evenly divided the driving, Sal should have driven 10 more miles.

6. Ryan has 8 more base hits than Joe has. Sean has 5 fewer hits than Manuel has. Joe has 10 hits, which is half as many hits as Manuel has.

   __T__ Manuel has more hits than the others.

   __T__ Sean has $1\frac{1}{2}$ as many hits as Joe.

   __F__ Ryan has 15 hits.

My, How You've Aged!

The graph shows changes in the median age of the United States population from 1800 to 1990. Use the graph to answer the questions.

1. What was the median age of the population in 1900?

about 23 years old

2. What was the median age of the population in 1840?

about 18 years old

3. For which two years was the median age the same?

1950 and 1980

4. By about how many years did the median age increase between the first and last dates shown on the graph?

by about 18 years

5. What does the graph indicate about median age of the population between 1800 and 1920?

The median age increased at a

steady rate between those

dates.

6. What does the graph indicate about the median age of the population between 1950 and 1970?

The median age of

the population declined

at a steady rate.

7. During which two 10-year spans did the median age change the most?

**from 1930 to 1940 and
from 1980 to 1990**

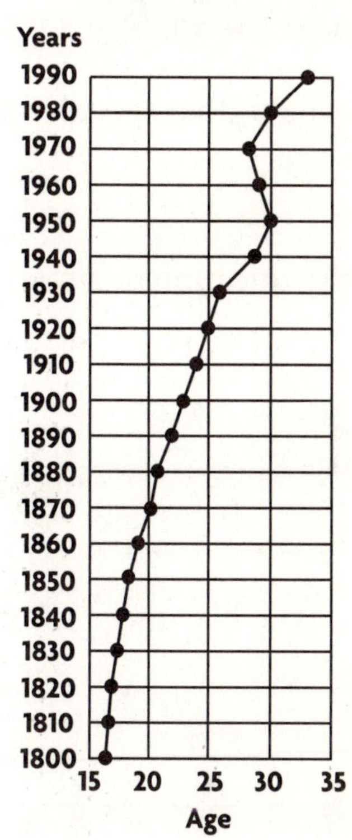

8. During which 10-year span did the median age remain almost constant?

between 1800 and 1810

9. What might have caused the change that occurred between 1950 and 1970?

**a disproportionate number of
births**

10. Based on the data from 1970 to 1990, predict the median age for 2000.

**It is likely the median age will be
greater than 35.**

STRETCH YOUR THINKING   E49

Bias in Advertising

Most advertisements try to persuade consumers to buy certain products. Some advertisements use biased surveys to make their products seem better than any others. Look carefully at advertisements shown in magazines and newspapers. Find an ad that includes either a biased question or a biased survey to promote a product. Answer these questions about the ad. **Answers will vary.**

1. What product does the advertisement feature? ______________________

   ____

2. How is the question or survey biased? ______________________

   ____

   ____

   ____

3. How does the bias make the product seem appealing? ______________

   ____

   ____

4. Describe two ways that the question or survey could be changed to

   eliminate the bias. ______________________________________

   ____

   ____

   ____

5. Explain why recognizing bias in advertisements will help you

   become a smart shopper. ______________________________

   ____

Video Game Survey

Marla surveyed sixth-grade students about the number of hours per week they spend playing video games. She organized her data in the graph below. Use the graph to answer the questions.

NUMBER OF HOURS SPENT PLAYING VIDEO GAMES PER WEEK

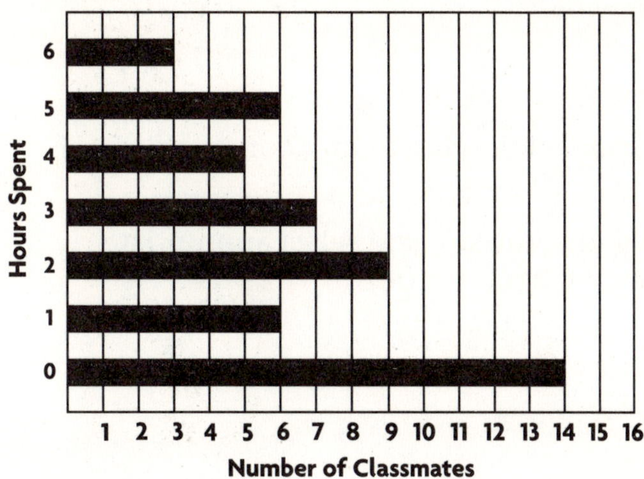

1. How many students did Marla survey?

   50 students

2. What is the range of her data?

   6

3. What fraction of the students surveyed spend 4 hours a week playing video games?

   $\frac{1}{10}$ **of the students**

4. What fraction of the students surveyed spend less than 2 hours a week playing video games?

   $\frac{2}{5}$ **of the students**

5. What fraction of the students surveyed spend more than 3 hours a week playing video games?

   $\frac{7}{25}$ **of the students**

6. For every 1 student who responded "6 hours," there were 2 students who responded "5 hours." What other pair of responses has a similar relationship?

   (1:2 ratio) 3 hr : 0 hr; 6 hr : 1 hr

7. Suppose Marla continued her survey and polled 100 additional classmates. Based on her first survey, how many students would likely respond "0 hours"?

   42 students

8. Suppose Marla wanted to expand her survey and ask another question about video game play. What are two possible questions she might ask?

   Possible answers: What is your favorite game? What type of system do you have?

Bar None

Use a yardstick or meterstick to measure the following distances, and complete the bar graph.

A. the width of your math book

B. the height of your desk

C. the length of this sheet of paper

D. the length of your pencil

E. the width of your desk

F. the height of the doorknob on the classroom door

Be sure to title the graph and both axes, and select appropriate intervals on the vertical axis. **Check students' graphs.**

Title: _______________________________

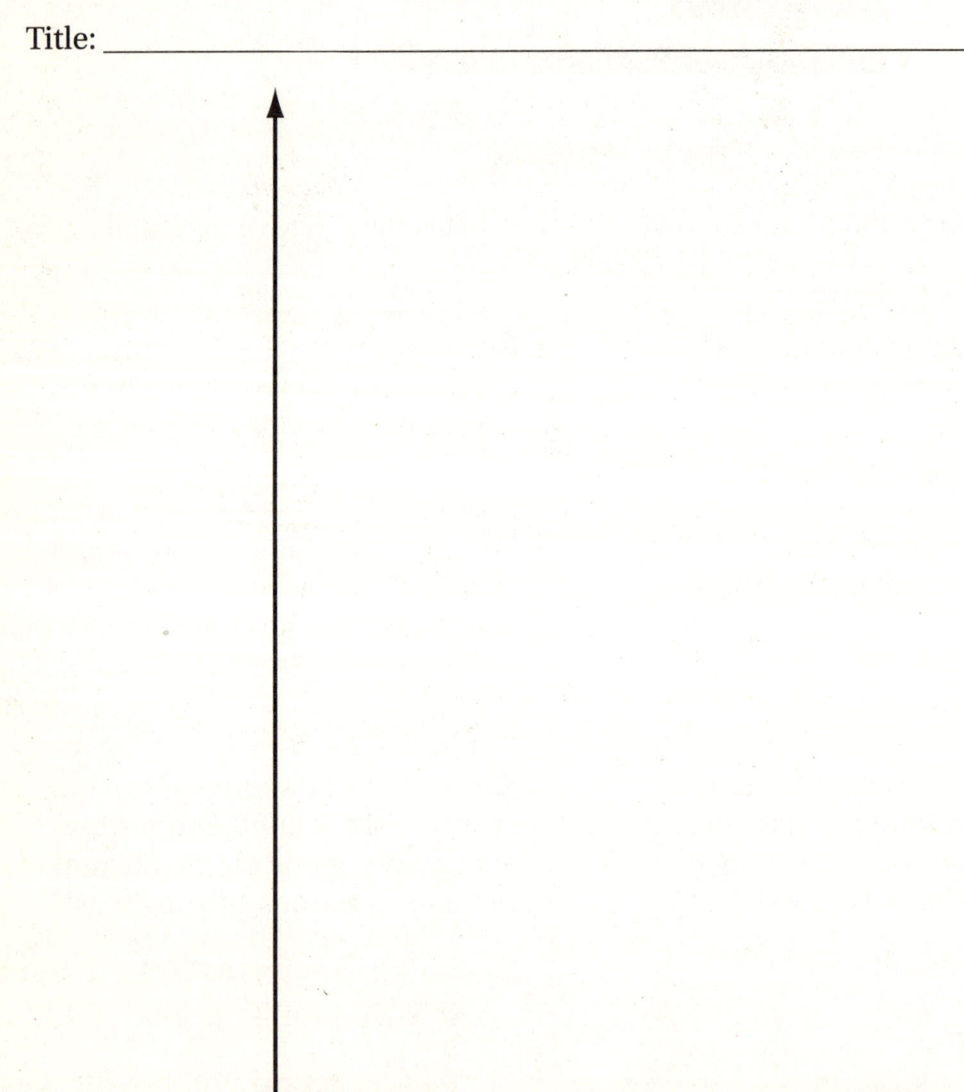

Play Ball!

The Ted Williams Middle School just finished their baseball season.
They played 20 games. Here are the results.

Game	1	2	3	4	5	6	7	8	9	10
Runs Scored by Williams	4	5	0	1	9	11	10	17	0	2
Runs Scored by Opponents	0	6	6	9	7	2	1	3	8	4

Game	11	12	13	14	15	16	17	18	19	20
Runs Scored by Williams	3	5	5	9	1	3	4	2	12	6
Runs Scored by Opponents	1	3	11	10	5	6	2	3	8	5

According to the table, Williams won their first game 4 to 0 and lost
game 13 by a score of 11 to 5.

You are the team's statistician. Answer each question.

1. What was the final record of the Ted Williams Middle School
baseball team for the season?

   10 wins, 10 losses

2. In a shut-out, a team scores no runs in the game. How many times
did Williams get shut out? How many times did Williams shut out
their opponent?

   2 times; 1 time

3. What was the average number of runs per game scored by Williams?

   5.45 runs

4. Complete the histogram showing runs
scored by Williams.

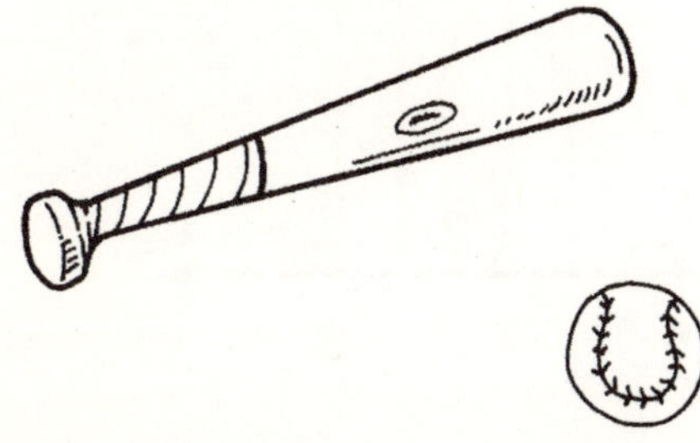

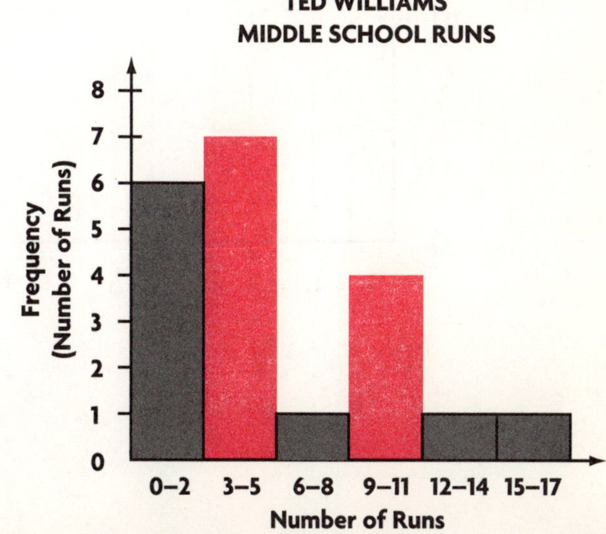

STRETCH YOUR THINKING   E53

No Business Like Snow Business

If you melt 8 or 10 in. of snow, you get only about 1 in. of water.
Snow can be wet and slushy, or it can be dry and powdery.
So, you can get 1 in. of water from 4 to 6 in. of wet snow or
from 15 to 18 in. of powdery snow.

Last winter, one northern city had 8 snowstorms.
The table gives the data.

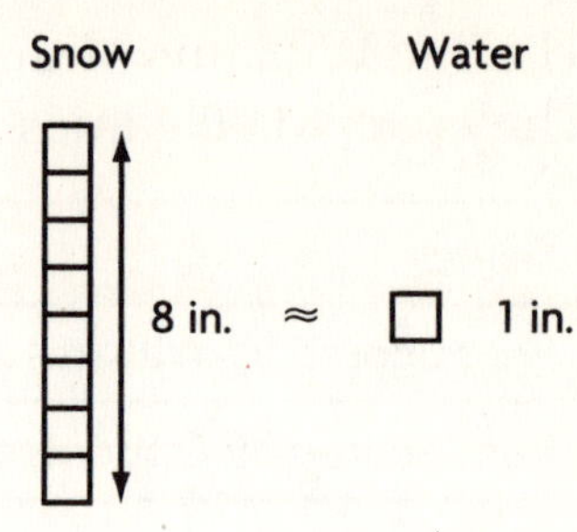

Storm	1	2	3	4	5	6	7	8
Snow (in.)	5	11	8	22	6	6	13	9
Melted Snow (in.)	1	1	1.5	2	0.5	1	1.5	1

1. Which storm was the wettest? _____the fourth_____

2. Which storm was the driest? _____the fifth_____

3. Make a double-bar graph to compare each snowfall with its
   water equivalent.

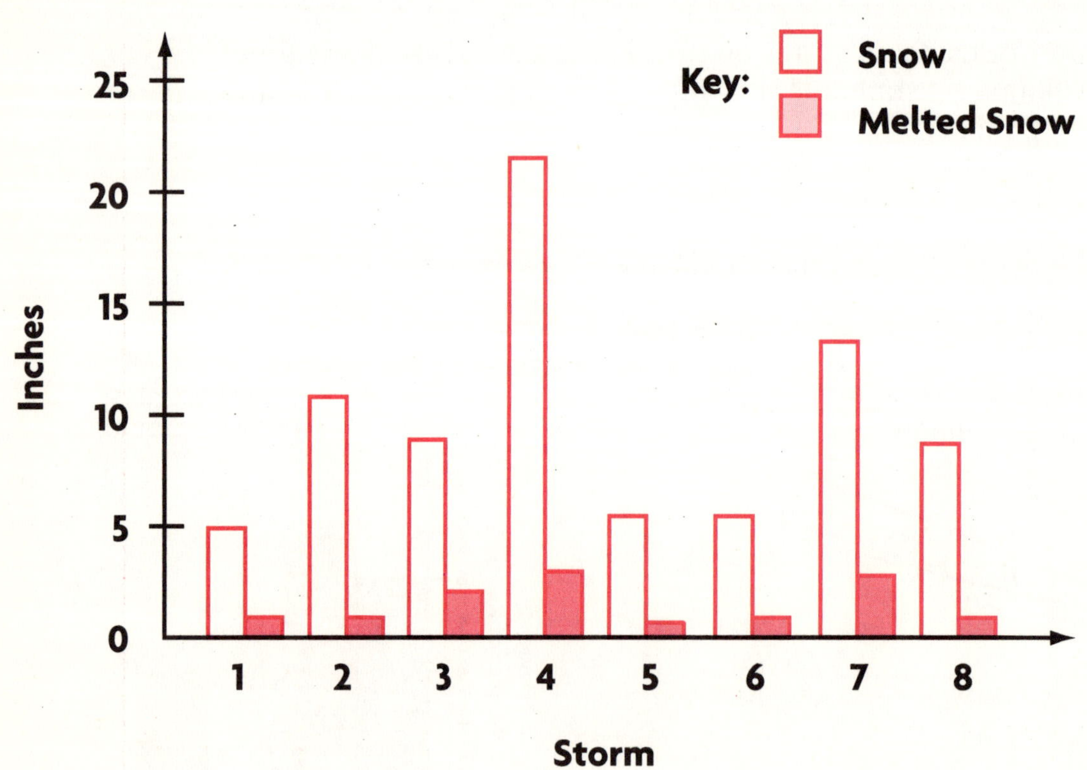

Around the Clock

There are 168 hours in a week. How do you spend your time during a typical week?

Complete the table. Add other categories if you wish. Be sure your total number of hours is 168. **Data will vary.**

How I spend a typical week	
Activity	**Hours**
At school	
Sleeping	
Eating meals	
Doing homework	
Playing	
Doing chores	
Other	

Use the circle below to make a circle graph to show how you spend your time. If you need to, round your angle measures to the nearest degree. **Check students' graphs.**

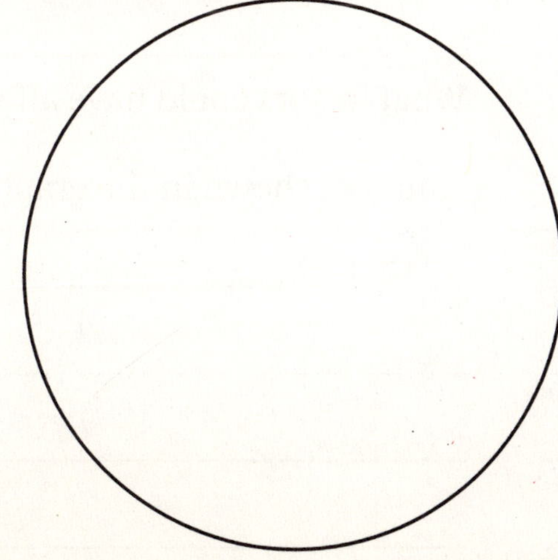

Analyzing Media Graphs

Newspapers and magazines often use graphs to provide information
to readers. Look through newspapers and magazines for examples of
two types of graphs. Then answer these questions about each graph.
If possible, attach the graphs to this paper.

Graphs and responses will vary. Check students' graphs.

Graph 1	**Graph 2**

Source: _______________________

Source: _______________________

Title of Graph: _______________

Title of Graph: _______________

Type of Graph: _______________

Type of Graph: _______________

What relationship does the graph show?

What relationship does the graph show?

____

____

____

____

____

____

What does an observer learn by viewing

What does an observer learn by viewing

the graph? ___________________

the graph? ___________________

____

____

____

____

____

____

____

____

What factors could have affected the

What factors could have affected the

variables shown in the graph? ________

variables shown in the graph? ________

____

____

____

____

____

____

Mislead the Consumer

Imagine that you own a snack food company. Your company has just created a new product called Tasty Treats. Your marketing department surveyed 100 people to determine which product they liked best. The results of the survey are shown in the table.

PRODUCT	RESPONSES
Crunchy Chips	36
Kracklin' Kernels	18
Nacho Nuggets	12
Power Pieces	10
Tasty Treats	24

In the space below, draw a graph to be used in an advertisement for Tasty Treats. Be sure to use the results of the survey to convince customers to buy your product. **Check students' graphs.**

How Many Television Sets?

The pictograph shows the number of households with television sets.
Use the pictograph to answer the questions.

1. How many households does each whole

   symbol represent ? _____**10 million**_____

2. How many households had television sets

   in 1950? _____**5 million**_____

3. How many households had television sets

   in 1980? _____**75 million**_____

4. How many more households had
   television sets in 1960 than in 1950?

   _____**40 million**_____

5. How many more households had
   television sets in 1980 than in 1970?

   _____**15 million**_____

**UNITED STATES: HOUSEHOLDS
WITH TELEVISION SETS**

1950
1960
1970
1980
1990

Each equals 10 million.

6. What is the difference in the numbers of households with
   television sets in the first and last years shown in the pictograph?

   _____**85 million more in 1990 than in 1950**_____

7. Do you see a trend in the data? Explain. _____**yes; since 1960, an**_____

   _____**increase of 15 million households with sets each decade**_____

8. From this trend, predict the number of households with

   television sets in 2000. _____**105 million**_____

9. How would this amount be represented in the pictograph?

   _____**10 whole sets and 1 half set**_____

10. Why are years prior to 1950 omitted from the pictograph?

    _____**TV was not available to consumers.**_____

Number Puzzles

Use the information to find the numbers in the group. The first one is done for you. **Possible answers are given.**

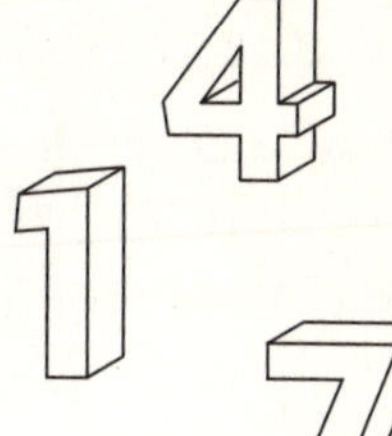

1. There are 7 whole numbers in a group. The least number in the group is 6. The greatest number in the group is 16. The mode of the group is 15. The median is 10 and the mean is 11.

   6, 7, 8, 10, 15, 15, 16

2. There are 5 whole numbers in a group. The least number is 7 and the greatest is 14. The mode is 9 and the median is 9. The mean is 10.

   7, 9, 9, 11, 14

3. There are 7 whole numbers in a group. The greatest number is 20 and the least is 8. The median is 12 and the mode is 12. The mean is 13.

   8, 10, 12, 12, 14, 15, 20

4. There are 7 whole numbers in a group. The least number is 5 and the greatest is 15. The mean and the median are 11. The mode is 15.

   5, 7, 9, 11, 15, 15, 15

5. There are 7 whole numbers in a group. The least number is 11 and the greatest is 17. The mean and the median are 14. There is no mode.

   11, 12, 13, 14, 15, 16, 17

6. There are 7 whole numbers in a group. The least number is 15 and the greatest is 33. The mean is 23. The median is 22. The mode is 19.

   15, 19, 19, 22, 25, 28, 33

7. There are 7 whole numbers in a group. The greatest number is 37 and the least is 21. The median is 29. The mean is 28. The mode is 31.

   21, 23, 24, 29, 31, 31, 37

Name the Amount!

Write your answer.

1. Sue received scores of 79, 83, 76, and 100 on her first four math tests. What score must she get on her fifth test to have an average of 85 for all five tests?

87

2. Kyle bowled scores of 112, 126, 98, and 118 in his first four games. What score must he bowl in his fifth game to have an average of 120 for all five games?

146

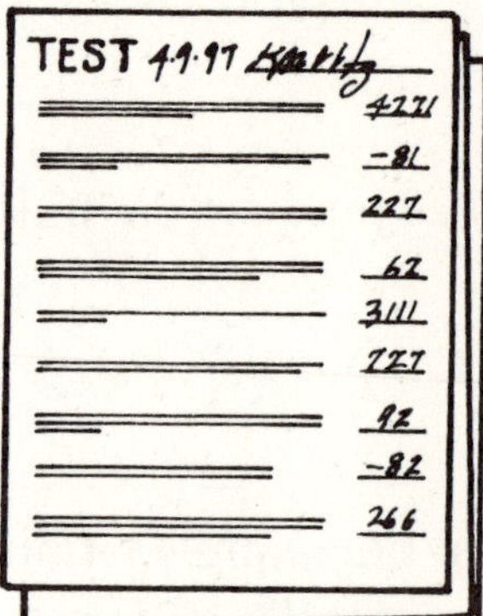

3. In his first five rounds of golf, Jon scored 84, 71, 77, 68, 74. What score must Jon achieve in his sixth round in order to have an average of 75 for all six rounds?

76

4. Matt scored 89, 93, 100, 77, and 81 on his first five science tests. What score must he earn on his sixth test in order to have an average of 90 for all six tests?

100

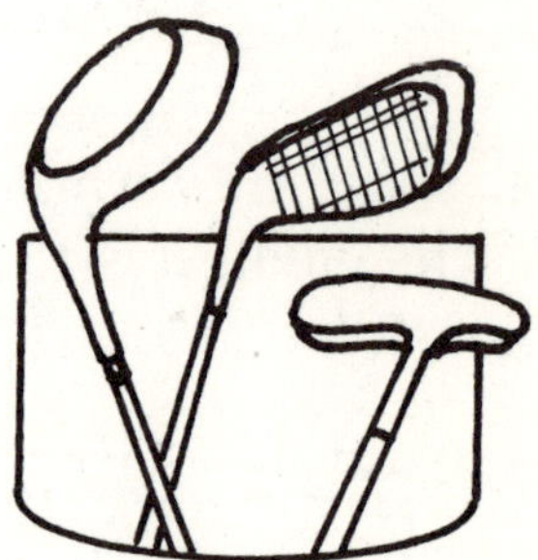

5. In her first five games, Betty bowled 128, 116, 104, 112, and 134. What must she bowl in her sixth game in order to have an average of 120 for all six games?

126

6. The following numbers of moviegoers saw the first six showings of a recently released movie: 213, 322, 278, 309, 258, 296. How many movie fans must attend the seventh showing in order to have an average of 280 people per showing?

284 people

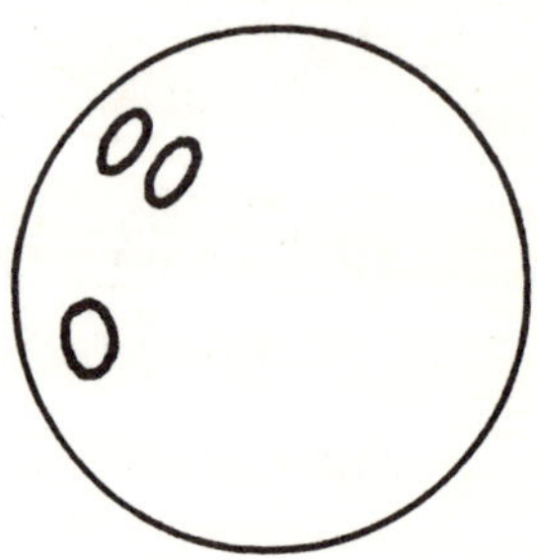

7. The following number of students went to the first five basketball games: 180, 200, 175, 200, 205. How many students must attend the sixth game in order to have an average of 200 students per game?

240 students

Polygon Percents

Express each area as a percent.

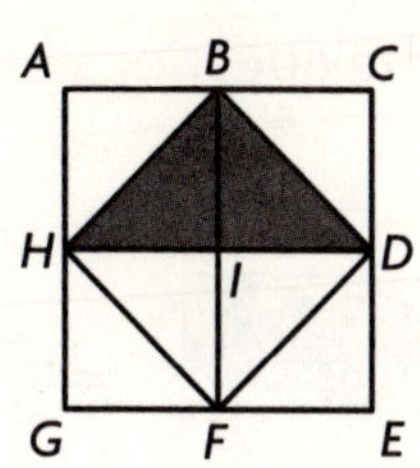

	SHADED AREA	**UNSHADED AREA**
1. Square *ACEG*	25%	75%
2. Rectangle *ACDH*	50%	50%
3. Trapezoid *BCDH*	$66\frac{2}{3}$%	$33\frac{1}{3}$%
4. Pentagon *BCDFH*	40%	60%
5. Rectangle *HDEG*	0%	100%
6. Pentagon *BCEFH*	$33\frac{1}{3}$%	$66\frac{2}{3}$%
7. Triangle *BHD*	100%	0%
8. Triangle *FHB*	50%	50%
9. Rectangle *CEFB*	25%	75%
10. Square *HIFG*	0%	100%
11. Square *ABIH*	50%	50%
12. Triangle *BID*	100%	0%

Find the Percent

Use the figures to answer the questions below.

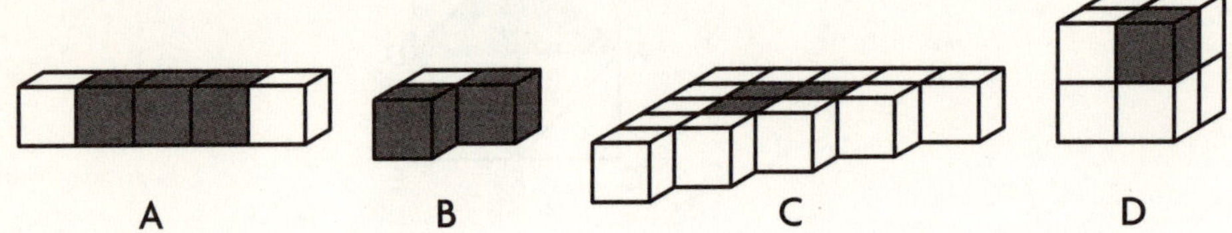

1. What percent of the cubes in Figure A are shaded? _____ **60%** _____

2. What percent of the cubes in Figure B are not shaded? _____ **$33\frac{1}{3}$%** _____

3. What percent of the cubes in Figure C are not shaded? _____ **80%** _____

4. What percent of the cubes in Figure D are shaded? _____ **12.5%** _____

5. What percent of the cubes in Figure A are not shaded? _____ **40%** _____

6. What percent of the cubes in Figure C are shaded? _____ **20%** _____

7. If a cube is picked at random from Figure A, what is the probability that it is

    shaded? not shaded? _____ **$\frac{3}{5}$, $\frac{2}{5}$** _____

8. If a cube is picked at random from among all the cubes in Figures A, B, C,

    and D, what is the probability that it is shaded? _____ **$\frac{9}{31}$** _____

Suppose a 1-ft segment represents 100%. Find the length of the
segment that represents the given percent of the whole.

9. 50% __**6-in. segment**__

10. 200% __**24-in. segment**__

11. 75% __**9-in. segment**__

12. 125% __**15-in. segment**__

13. 350% __**42-in. segment**__

14. 275% __**33-in. segment**__

15. 25% __**3-in. segment**__

16. 150% __**18-in. segment**__

17. $33\frac{1}{3}$% __**4-in. segment**__

18. $133\frac{1}{3}$% __**16-in. segment**__

Figure Fun

Look at each figure. Estimate the percent of the figure that is shaded.
Possible estimates are given.

1. Figure A ______ **25%** ______

2. Figure B ______ **25%** ______

3. Figure C ______ **75%** ______

4. Figure D ______ **25%** ______

5. Figure E ______ **30%** ______

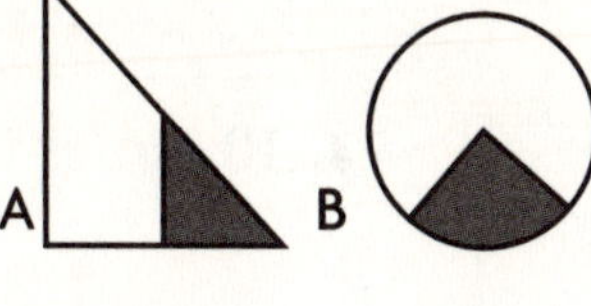
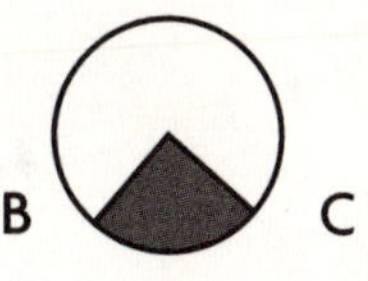
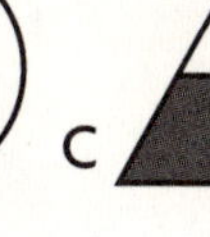
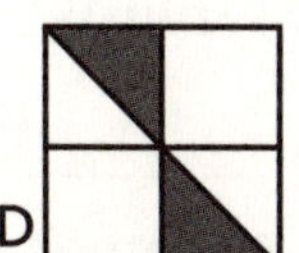
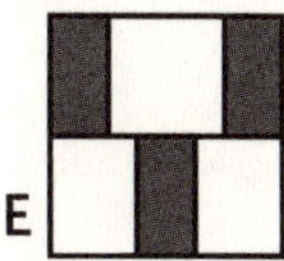

Suppose a dart lands on each figure at random. Estimate the probability
that it lands in a shaded area.

6. Figure A ______ $\frac{1}{4}$ ______

7. Figure B ______ $\frac{1}{4}$ ______

8. Figure C ______ $\frac{3}{4}$ ______

9. Figure D ______ $\frac{1}{4}$ ______

10. Figure E ______ $\frac{3}{10}$ ______

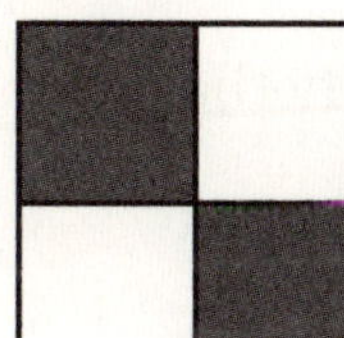
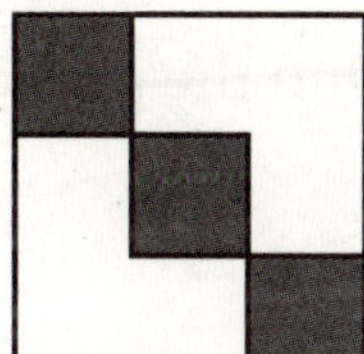
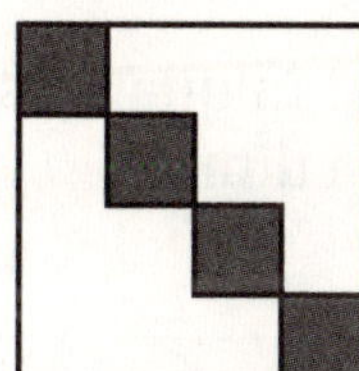
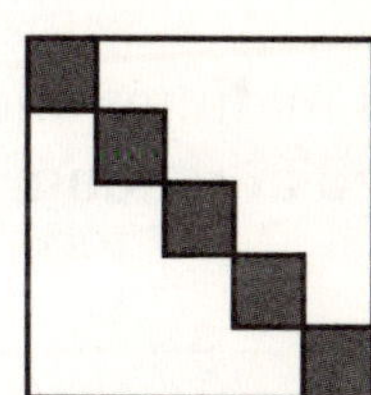

Start	Stage 1	Stage 2	Stage 3	Stage 4

Use the sequence of figures to answer the questions below.

11. If the large shaded square represents 1, what fractional part of the
square is shaded in Stage 1?

$\frac{1}{2}$

12. What fractional part of the square is shaded in Stage 2? Stage 3?
Stage 4?

$\frac{1}{3}, \frac{1}{4}, \frac{1}{5}$

13. Stage 5 is not shown. What fractional part of the square would be
shaded in Stage 5?

$\frac{1}{6}$

Comparing Coins

Write a ratio that compares the dollar values of the two sets of coins.

1. 5 dimes to 6 quarters

   1:3

2. 16 nickels to 2 dimes

   4:1

3. 6 quarters to 6 nickels

   5:1

4. 10 dimes to 20 quarters

   1:5

5. 3 nickels to 3 quarters

   1:5

6. 1 quarter to 20 dimes

   1:8

7. 9 quarters to 15 nickels

   3:1

8. 48 dimes to 12 nickels

   8:1

9. 5 quarters to 1 nickel

   25:1

10. 11 pennies to 11 quarters

    1:25

11. 7 nickels to 21 dimes

    1:6

12. 30 nickels to 3 dimes

    5:1

Solve.

13. You have $3 in dimes and $3 in quarters. Find the probability that a coin picked at random is a dime.

    $$\frac{5}{7}$$

14. You have $1 in pennies, $1 in nickels, and $1 in dimes. Find the probability that a coin picked at random is worth more than 2 cents.

    $$\frac{3}{13}$$

15. You have $2 in nickels and $2 in quarters. Find the probability that a coin picked at random is a dime.

    0

Expression Match

Write an algebraic expression for "a number, *n*, less than seven,
all divided by 2."

$(7 - n) \div 2$

• The 7 must come first, because *n* is less than 7.
• To show "all divided by 2," use parentheses.

Draw a line connecting the word expression in Column 1 to the correct
algebraic expression in Column 2.

Column 1

1. twenty-two less than a number, *a*, all times three

2. twenty-two times a number, *a*, plus three

3. a number, *a*, increased by three, all times twenty-two

4. a number, *a*, decreased by twenty-two, all divided by three

5. twenty-two times a number, *a*, decreased by three

6. a number, *a*, divided by three, increased by twenty-two

7. the sum of three and twenty-two, all divided by a number, *a*

8. a number, *a*, less than twenty-two, all times three

9. the sum of a number, *a*, and three, all divided by twenty-two.

10. a number, *a*, decreased by three and then increased by twenty-two

Column 2

A. $a \div 3 + 22$

B. $a - 3 + 22$

C. $22 \times a + 3$

D. $(a - 22) \times 3$

E. $(22 - a) \times 3$

F. $(a - 22) \div 3$

G. $(a + 3) \div 22$

H. $(a + 3) \times 22$

I. $22 \times a - 3$

J. $(3 + 22) \div a$

Lost and Found

For each value under owners, there are
two algebraic expressions that evaluate to
the same answer. In the example, $a + 3$ and
$7 - a$ both have the same answer of 5 when
$a = 2$. So, $a + 3$ and $7 - a$ both belong to $a = 2$.

Example
$a = 2$
$a + 3 = 2 + 3 = 5$
$7 - a = 7 - 2 = 5$

Find the two lost algebraic puppies and return
them to their owners. To do this, circle the two
algebraic expressions that evaluate to the same answer.

Owners   **Algebraic Puppies**

1. $a = 5$

2. $a = 6$

3. $a = 7$

4. $a = 8$

What's My Input?

Leonard only recorded certain parts for each input-output table.
Complete the missing parts of each table.

1.

Input	Algebraic Expression	Output
d	$d \times 2 + 3$	
a. 2	$2 \times 2 + 3$	7
b. 5	$5 \times 2 + 3$	13
c. 8	$8 \times 2 + 3$	19
d. 10	$10 \times 2 + 3$	23
e. 12	$12 \times 2 + 3$	27
f. 15	$15 \times 2 + 3$	33
g. 18	$18 \times 2 + 3$	39
h. 20	$20 \times 2 + 3$	43
i. 24	$24 \times 2 + 3$	51
j. 30	$30 \times 2 + 3$	63
k. 36	$36 \times 2 + 3$	75
l. 44	$44 \times 2 + 3$	91
m. 52	$52 \times 2 + 3$	107
n. 88	$88 \times 2 + 3$	179
o. 120	$120 \times 2 + 3$	243
p. 140	$140 \times 2 + 3$	283
q. 200	$200 \times 2 + 3$	403
r. 260	$260 \times 2 + 3$	523
s. 340	$340 \times 2 + 3$	683
t. 450	$450 \times 2 + 3$	903

2.

Input	Algebraic Expression	Output
f	$f^2 - 4$	
a. 2	$2^2 - 4$	0
b. 3	$3^2 - 4$	5
c. 4	$4^2 - 4$	12
d. 5	$5^2 - 4$	21
e. 6	$6^2 - 4$	32
f. 10	$10^2 - 4$	96
g. 11	$11^2 - 4$	117
h. 12	$12^2 - 4$	140
i. 15	$15^2 - 4$	221
j. 18	$18^2 - 4$	320
k. 20	$20^2 - 4$	396
l. 24	$24^2 - 4$	572
m. 28	$28^2 - 4$	780
n. 30	$30^2 - 4$	896
o. 40	$40^2 - 4$	1,596
p. 44	$44^2 - 4$	1,932
q. 50	$50^2 - 4$	2,496
r. 52	$52^2 - 4$	2,700
s. 60	$60^2 - 4$	3,596
t. 70	$70^2 - 4$	4,896

STRETCH YOUR THINKING   E67

Balancing Act

Study the first two scales. Then answer the question to find what
is needed to balance the third scale.

1.

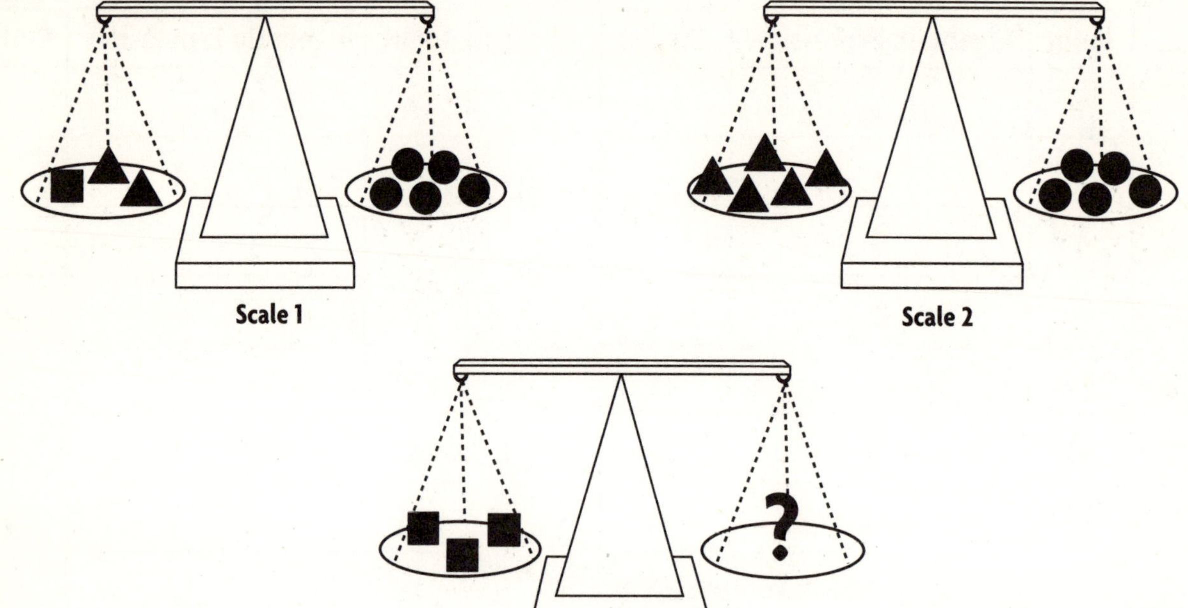

How many circles are needed to balance the 3 squares? _________ **9 circles**

2.

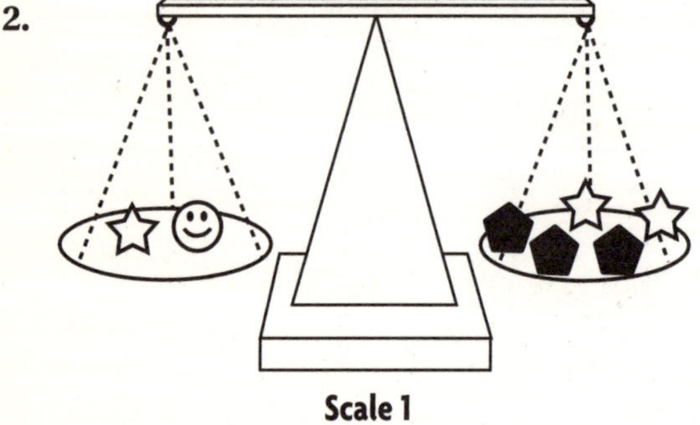

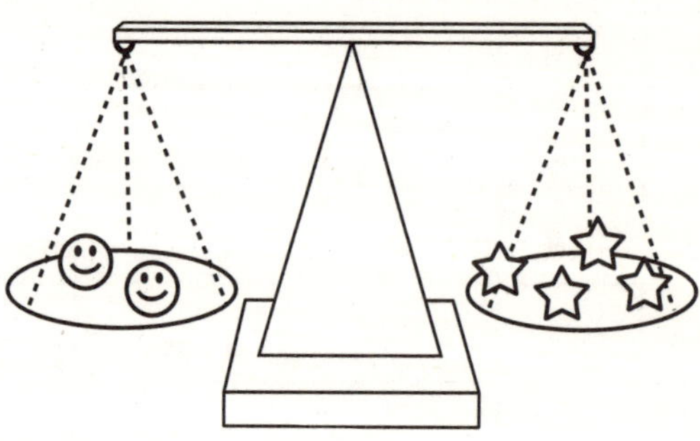

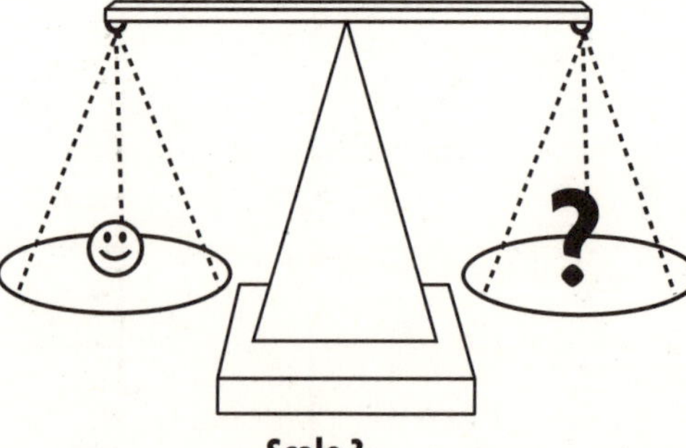

How many pentagons are needed to balance the 1 smiling face? _____ **6 pentagons**

E68   STRETCH YOUR THINKING

A Spotty Riddle

Solve each equation. Then put the letter of the variable above its value to answer the riddle.

$\dfrac{b}{2} = 5;\ b =$ __**10**__ $\qquad\qquad$ $\dfrac{r}{3} = 3;\ r =$ __**9**__

$3g = 6;\ g =$ __**2**__ $\qquad\qquad$ $2f = 10;\ f =$ __**5**__

$\dfrac{i}{4} = 3;\ i =$ __**12**__ $\qquad\qquad$ $\dfrac{m}{5} = 3;\ m =$ __**15**__

$3o = 18;\ o =$ __**6**__ $\qquad\qquad$ $3y = 9;\ y =$ __**3**__

$\dfrac{n}{2} = 8;\ n =$ __**16**__ $\qquad\qquad$ $\dfrac{v}{4} = 2;\ v =$ __**8**__

$4l = 16;\ l =$ __**4**__ $\qquad\qquad$ $2c = 14;\ c =$ __**7**__

$\dfrac{p}{2} = 7;\ p =$ __**14**__ $\qquad\qquad$ $\dfrac{a}{3} = 6;\ a =$ __**18**__

$\dfrac{t}{5} = 4;\ t =$ __**20**__ $\qquad\qquad$ $\dfrac{e}{2} = 11;\ e =$ __**22**__

How does a leopard change its spots?

b	y		m	o	v	i	n	g
10	3		15	6	8	12	16	2

f	r	o	m		p	l	a	c	e
5	9	6	15		14	4	18	7	22

t	o		p	l	a	c	e
20	6		14	4	18	7	22

STRETCH YOUR THINKING   E69

Can You Spare a Dime?

Circle the correct answer. Check your answer by using real coins.

1. Which circle is the size of a dime?

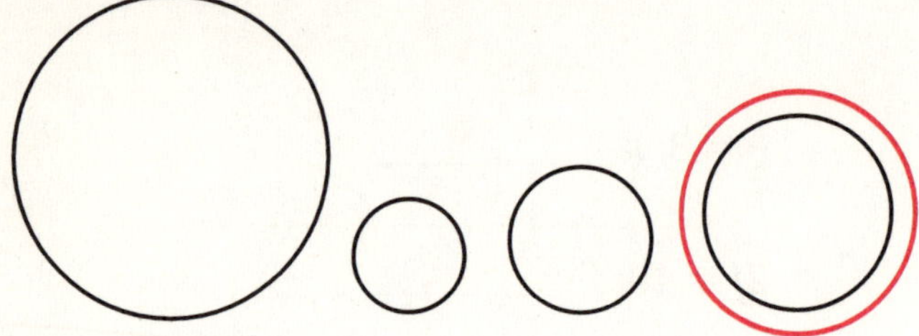

2. Which circle is the size of a nickel?

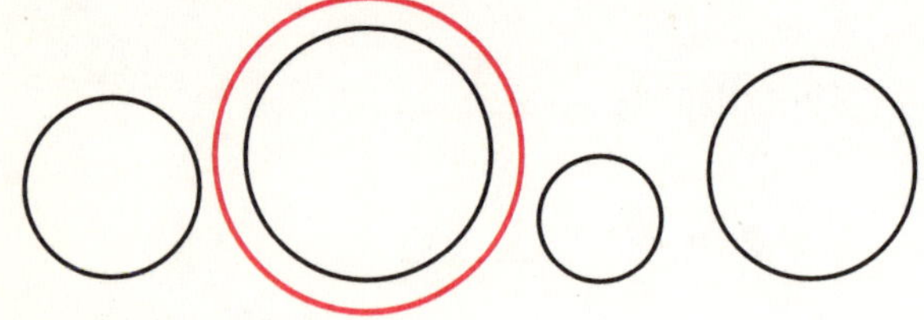

3. Which circle is the size of a quarter?

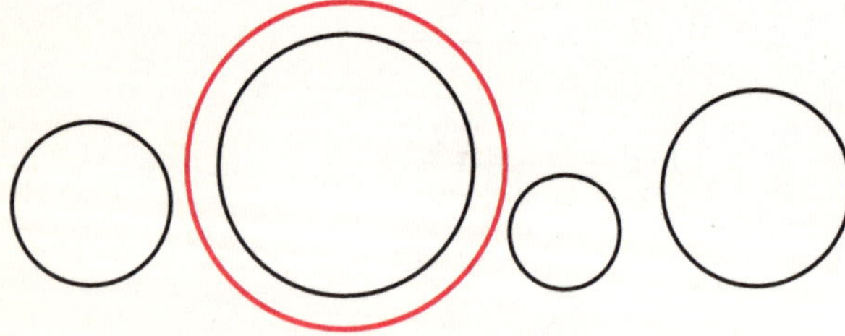

Estimate. **Students' estimates may vary.**

4. About how high would a stack of 100 pennies be?

   about 6 in.

5. About how high would a stack of 10,000 pennies be?

   about 50 ft

6. Estimate the number of pennies that will fit in the glass to the right.

   about 200 pennies

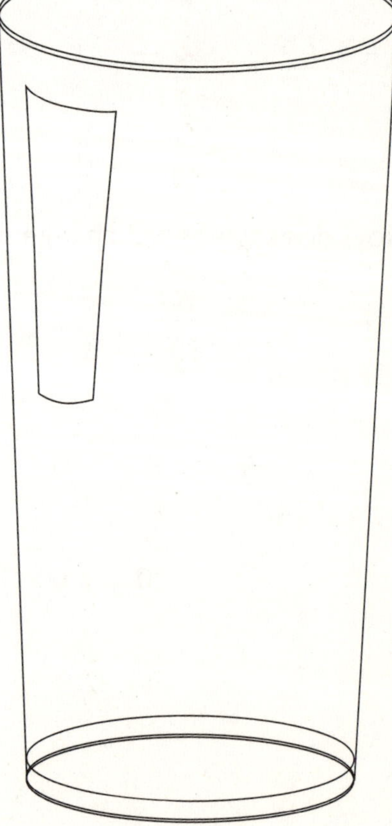

Get the Message?

Complete.

Then write the letters that go with your answers in the rows at the right.

If your answers are correct, the letters in the columns will spell a message.

Message

1. V	G	W
2. E	O	O
3. R	O	R
4. Y	D	K

1. A normal nighttime temperature in New York City in January is

   25°C (Write *GLP.*)   25°F (Write *VGW.*)   60°F (Write *ADF.*)

   VGW

2. An ice cube does not melt until the temperature goes above

   0°C (Write *EOO.*)   100°C (Write *PSR.*)   32°C (Write *OAI.*)

   EOO

3. The temperature at which water boils is

   212°C (Write *STA.*)   100°F (Write *OLG.*)   212°F (Write *ROR.*)

   ROR

4. On a windy summer day in San Francisco, a typical temperature might be

   60°C (Write *OYN.*)   98°F (Write *EST.*)   60°F (Write *YDK.*)

   YDK

Make a Spiral

Pilots use vectors to show both direction and distance.
Draw a vector as an arrow.

Draw the vector (9, 30°).

- Measure 30° counterclockwise from 0°.
- Draw an arrow 9 units long from the center of the circle.
- Label the angle and the vector.

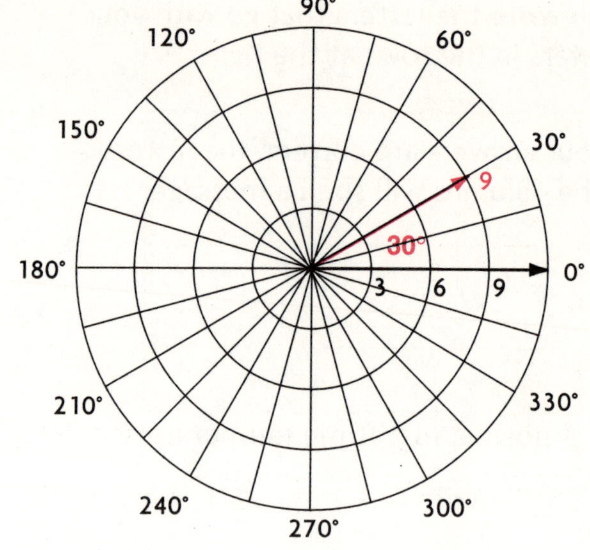

Draw each vector. When you finish, you will have made a spiral.

1. (8, 180°)	**2.** (3, 30°)	**3.** (4, 60°)	**4.** (9, 210°)
5. (5, 90°)	**6.** (12, 300°)	**7.** (11, 270°)	**8.** (6, 120°)
9. (7, 150°)	**10.** (13, 330°)	**11.** (14, 0°)	**12.** (10, 240°)

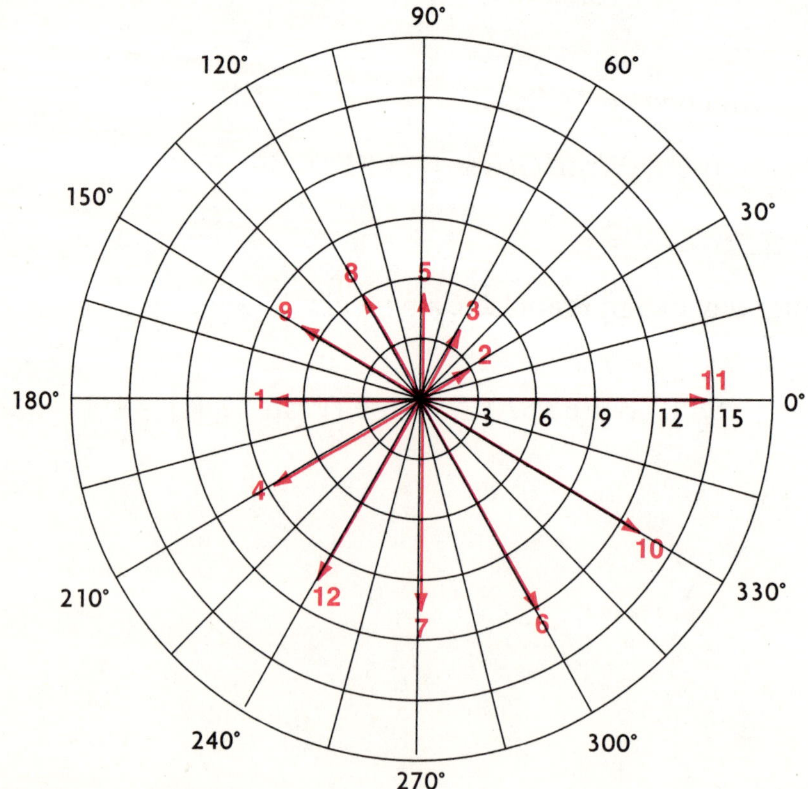

For Good Measure

Use your calculator to complete each table.

1.

Inches	Centimeters
0.1	**0.254**
1	2.54
60	**152.4**
300	**762**

2.

Liters	Quarts
0.1	**0.1057**
1	1.057
10	**10.57**
200	**211.4**

3.

Grams	Ounces
1	0.035
20	**0.7**
60	**2.1**
350	**12.25**

4.

Meters	Inches
0.2	**7.874**
1	39.37
8	**314.96**
35	**1,377.95**

Use the tables to help you estimate each answer. Round to the nearest tenth.

5. A bowl of cereal contains 6 grams of sugar. About how many ounces of sugar are in the bowl of cereal?

about 0.2 oz of sugar

6. Janine buys 5 liters of soda for a party. About how many quarts of soda does she buy?

about 5.3 qt

7. A picture measures 8 in. × 10 in. Estimate the dimensions of the picture, in centimeters.

about 20.3 cm × 25.4 cm

8. Sound travels at a speed of 331.82 meters per second. About how many inches per second does sound travel?

about 13,063.8 in. per sec

9. A newborn baby weighs about 3,500 grams. About how many ounces does a newborn baby weigh?

about 122.5 oz

10. A snake is 40 centimeters long. About how many inches long is the snake?

about 15.7 in. long

11. Jake is 62 in. tall. About how many meters tall is Jake?

about 1.6 m tall

12. About how many liters are 10 gallons of gas?

about 37.8 L

What Are the Odds?

People often use *odds* to describe how likely it is that something will occur. Odds are ratios. Drawing a diagram can help you picture what is meant by odds.

- The radio reports, "The odds against rain today are 2 to 1." You can draw a diagram like this, showing 1 "rain" for every 2 "no rains."

RAIN	NO RAIN	NO RAIN

There is a chance of rain. But it is *twice as likely* that it *won't* rain. The odds are 2:1 against rain, and 1:2 for rain.

- Jake tossed a coin five times. Each time *heads* came up. Before the next toss, he states, "The next toss will *have* to be *tails*. It can't be *heads* again, can it? What are the odds?"

Draw a diagram for *each* toss.

HEADS	TAILS

The coin doesn't "remember" that there have been five *heads* in a row. All that matters is that on the sixth toss, it will be either *heads* or *tails*. Tell Jake that the odds are 50:50 ("fifty-fifty"), or 1 to 1, that heads will come up.

Give the odds.

1. The weather report states that there is a "one in four" chance of snow. Find the odds against snow.

   3 to 1

2. Jane rolls a number cube with numbers 1, 2, 3, 4, 5, and 6. What are the odds against her getting a 6?

   5 to 1

3. There are eight teams in the play-offs, and all eight are equally good. What are the odds against a team winning?

   7 to 1

4. Mr. Harris's house faces the ball field. There are three windows on that side, two ordinary ones and one expensive stained-glass window. All three are the same size. If Hal hits a ball and breaks a window, what are the odds that he breaks the expensive window?

   1:2 in favor; 2:1 against

Pathfinder

There is just one path from the top row to the bottom row where the rates are equal at each step. Find the path.

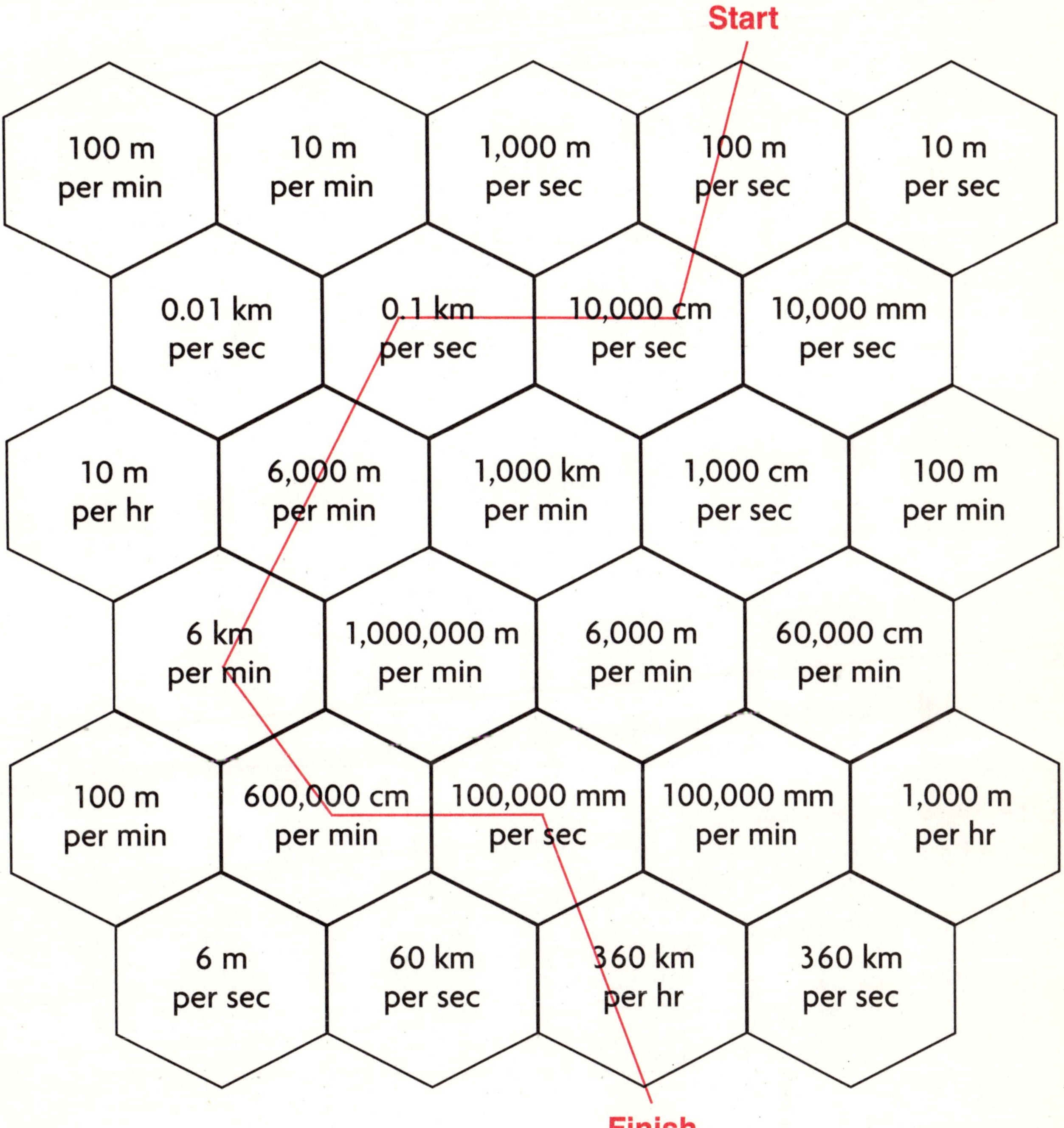

Strange Dimensions

Find the perimeter of each rectangle. First, however, you need to
change the percents to fractions or decimals.

1.

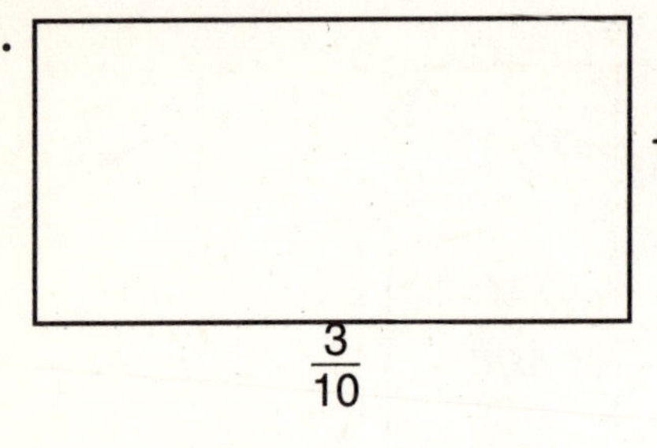

$\frac{8}{10}$

____

2.

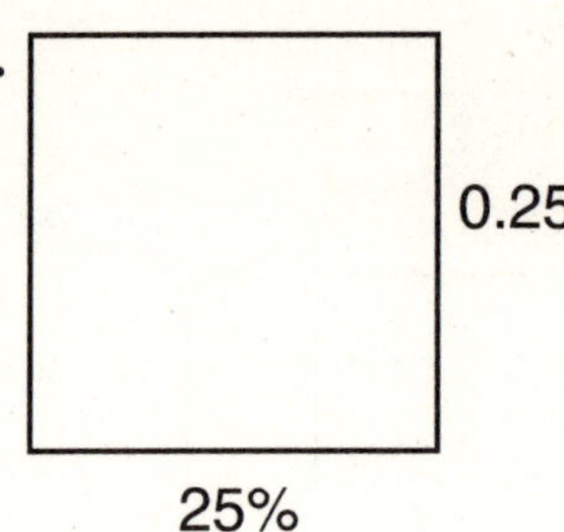

1

____

3.

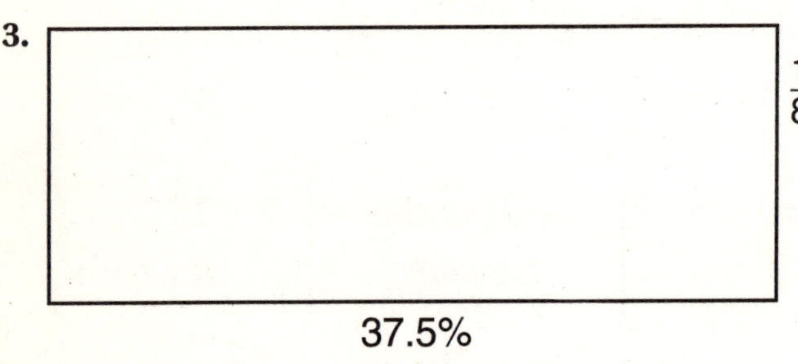

1

____

4.

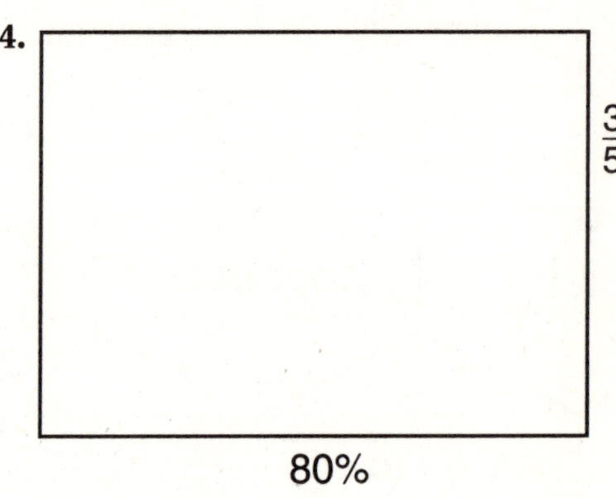

$2\frac{4}{5}$

____

5.

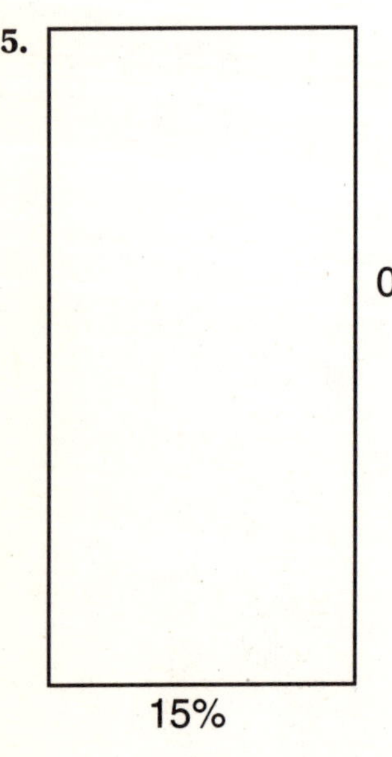

0.9

____

6.

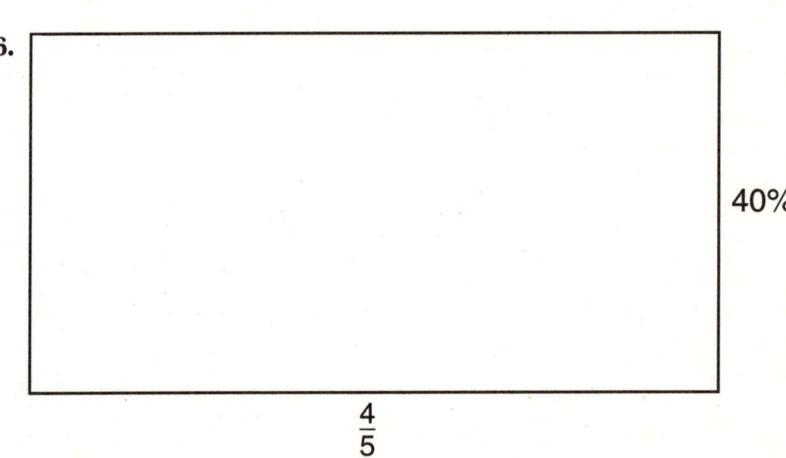

$2\frac{2}{5}$

____

E76 **STRETCH YOUR THINKING**

In the Shade

Estimate what percent of each figure is shaded.
Then measure by using an inch or centimeter ruler, and calculate the percent that is shaded.

1. 

2. 

Estimate: **Answers will vary.**

Actual: **20%**

Estimate: **Answers will vary.**

Actual: **75%**

3. In the space below, draw a rectangle and shade 30% of it. Then draw a circle and shade $66\frac{2}{3}$% of it. **Check students' drawings.**

rectangle   circle

The Value of a Dollar

	Britain	Canada	China	Israel	Japan	Mexico
Foreign Currency in U.S. Dollars	1.62	0.73	0.12	0.3	0.008	0.13
1 Dollar in Foreign Currency	0.62	1.36	8.32	3.34	124.46	7.76

The chart shows the recent values of various currencies compared with that of the U.S. dollar. For example:

- A Canadian dollar is worth $0.73 in U.S. dollars, while a U.S. dollar is worth 1.36 Canadian dollars.
- A Mexican peso is worth 13 cents in U.S. dollars, while a U.S. dollar is worth 7.76 Mexican pesos.

(Note: The numbers in the chart change every day. See the business section of a newspaper for today's rates.)

Solve.

1. You have $100 in U.S. dollars. How many units of local currency are worth this amount in each country?

Britain	**62**	Canada	**136**
China	**832**	Israel	**334**
Japan	**12,446**	Mexico	**776**

2. You return from Japan with 1,000 yen. What is this worth in U.S. dollars?

$8.00

3. A dime is worth about how many Mexican pesos?

about 0.776 pesos

4. A quarter is worth about how many Japanese yen?

about 31.115 yen

5. You make a purchase, and receive two quarters in change. Would you prefer that the coins be U.S. or Canadian? Why?

Answers will vary. U.S. quarters are worth more than

Canadian quarters.

Divide and Conquer

To find a percent of a number, you can divide the number into
equal groups.

To find 20% of the number of pennies, dividing them into groups of
10 helps.

This is because $10 \times 10\% = 100\%$. So, 20% of 20 pennies is 4 pennies,
or two groups.

Use the idea of dividing into equal groups to answer each question.

1. Find 5% of the circles below by dividing them into 20 equal groups.
   $20 \times 5\% = 100\%$

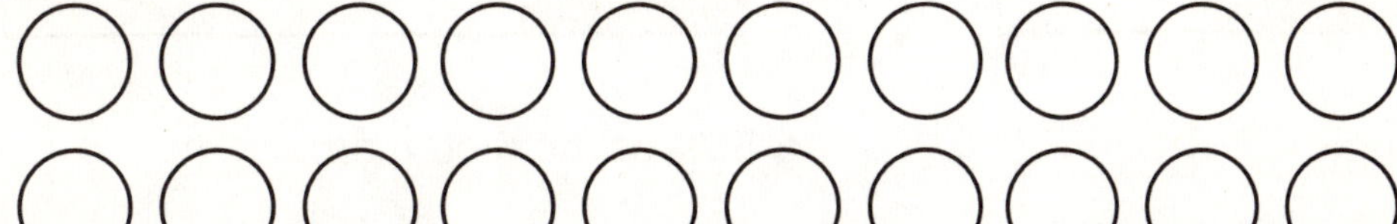

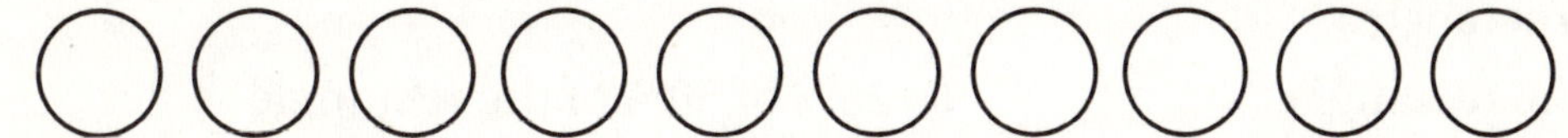

____**3 circles**____

2. Find 15% of the rectangles below by dividing them into 20 equal
   groups. $20 \times 5\% = 100\%$

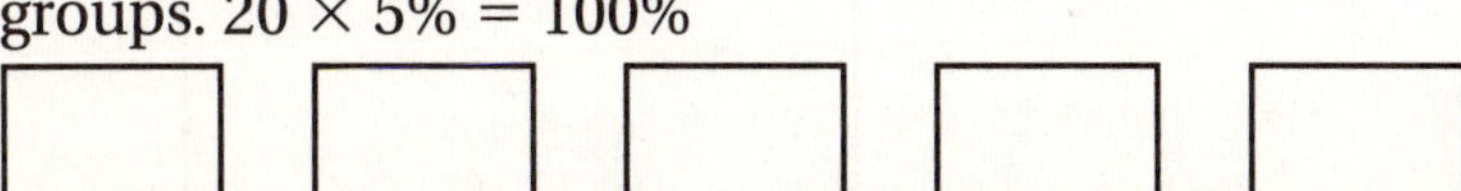

____**1.5 rectangles**____

STRETCH YOUR THINKING   E79

Shady Percents?

You can show 40% of a rectangle by writing it as a fraction.

$$40\% = 0.40 = \frac{40}{100} = \frac{4}{10} = \frac{2}{5}$$

Then use the fraction to shade the rectangle.

For each exercise, shade the rectangle.

1. 70% of the rectangle

2. 30% of the rectangle

3. 25% of the rectangle

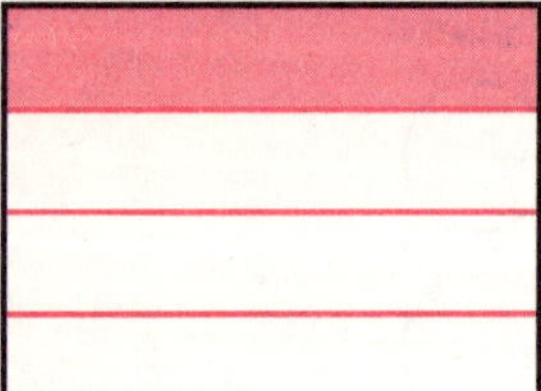

4. 55% of the rectangle

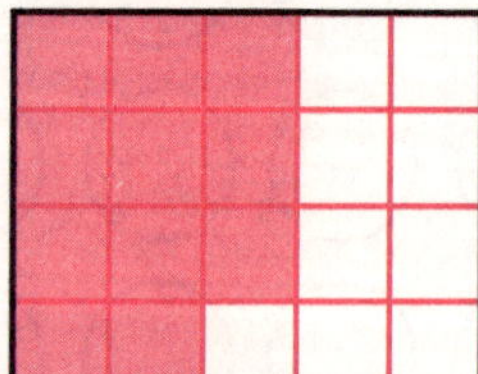

Taking percents of percents is done by working right to left. For each exercise, shade the rectangle.

5. 50% of 25% of the rectangle

6. 25% of 50% of the rectangle

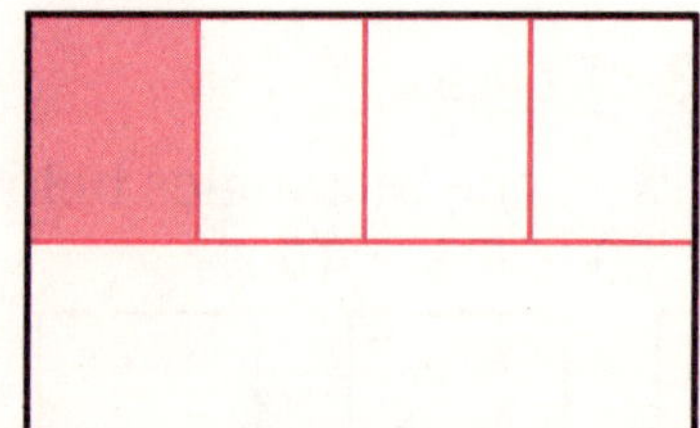

 STRETCH YOUR THINKING

Bits and Pieces

Sometimes when you make a circle graph, you may need to round the
angle measure for a section to the nearest degree.

For example,

47% of $360° = 0.47 \times 360° = 169.2° = 169°$

Lance made two circle graphs and labeled them with either percents or
the number of degrees. He then cut out the two circle graphs and all of
the pieces to paste them on a poster. He got all of the pieces mixed up.
Help him put the pieces back into the right graph.

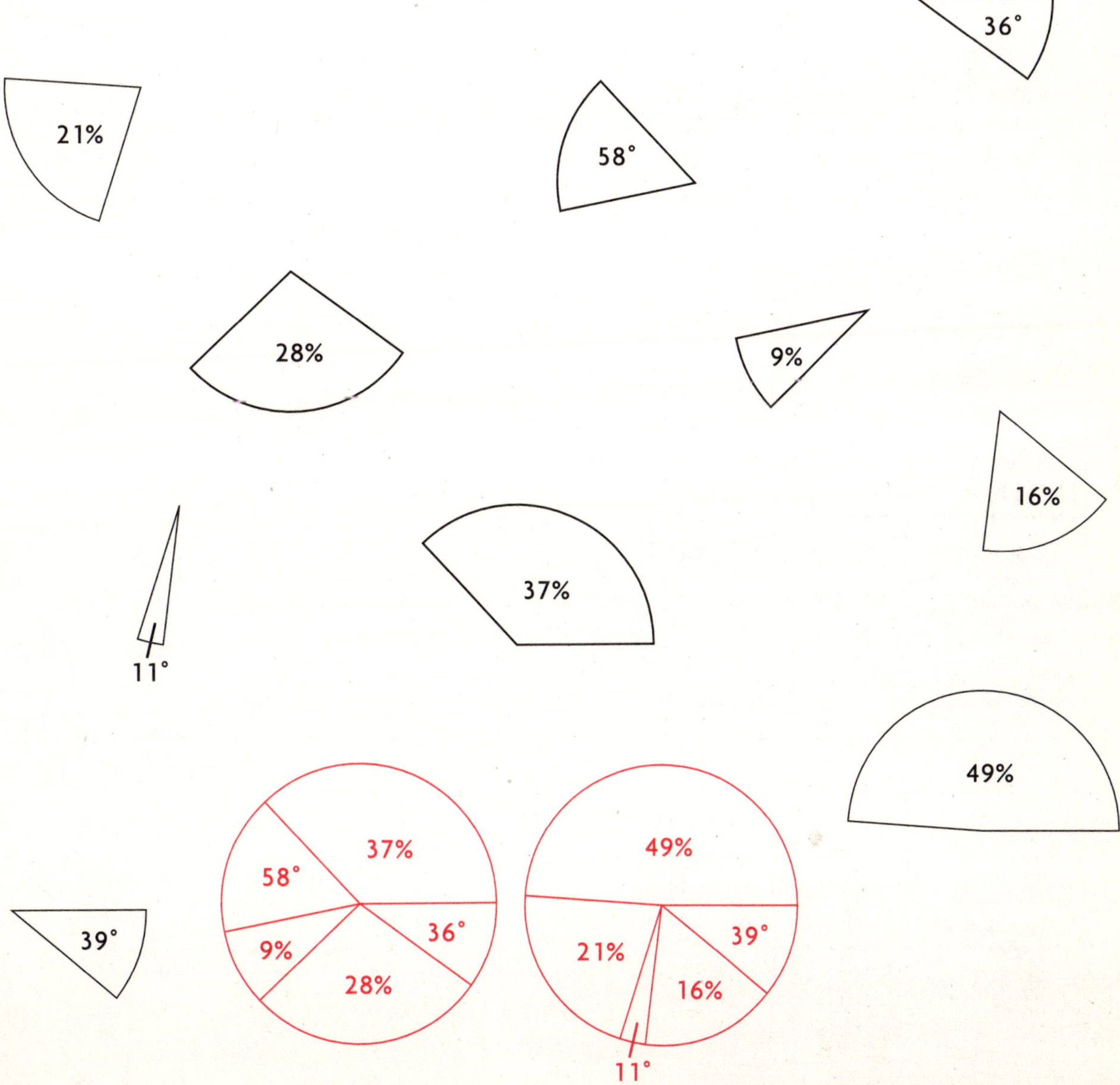

STRETCH YOUR THINKING   E81

Better Buy

Offering discounts helps stores attract customers. Smart customers compare the discounts to see which store is offering the better buy.

Decide which store has the better buy.

1.

__________**Store A**__________

2.

__________**Store B**__________

3.

__________**Store B**__________

4.

__________**Store B**__________

More Interest, Please!

When you deposit money in a bank, you receive interest. The bank even pays you interest on the interest they paid you.

If you invest $1,000 for two years at 5%, the bank calculates your interest in the following manner:

End of Year 1

$1,000 × 0.05 = $50.00 interest

So, you have $1,000 + $50 = $1,050 in the bank.

End of Year 2

$1,050 × 0.05 = $52.50

So, you have $1,050 + $52.50 = $1,102.50 in the bank.

This is called compound interest.

Use a calculator to find the amount in the bank for each amount, using compound interest. Round to the nearest cent where necessary.

1. Principal: $3,000

   Rate: 5%

   Years: 2

   _____ **$3,307.50** _____

2. Principal: $5,000

   Rate: 5%

   Years: 3

   _____ **$5,788.13** _____

3. Principal: $7,000

   Rate: 6%

   Years: 4

   _____ **$8,837.34** _____

4. Principal: $8,000

   Rate: 7%

   Years: 4

   _____ **$10,486.36** _____

5. Principal: $12,000

   Rate: 7%

   Years: 5

   _____ **$16,830.63** _____

6. Principal: $18,000

   Rate: 6.8%

   Years: 4

   _____ **$23,418.41** _____

7. Principal: $24,587

   Rate: 3.5%

   Years: 10

   _____ **$34,682.39** _____

8. Principal: $100,000

   Rate: 9.5%

   Years: 10

   _____ **$247,822.78** _____

STRETCH YOUR THINKING   E83

Odd Figure Out

Select the figure that is not similar to the rest.

1.

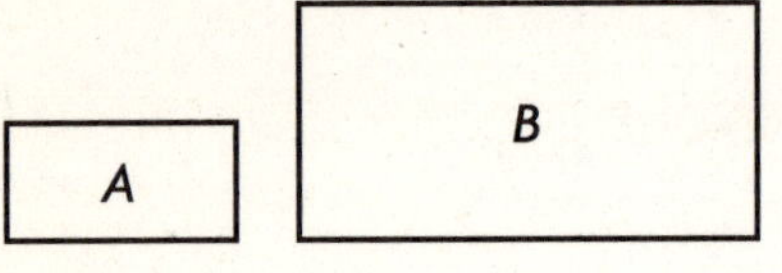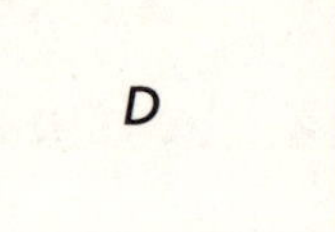

__________ **D**

2.

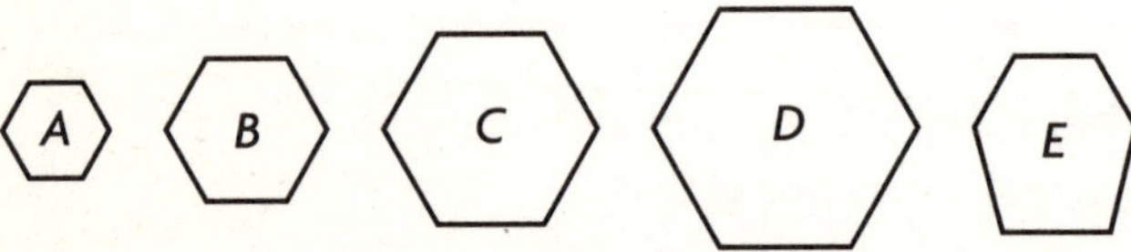

__________ **A**

3.

__________ **E**

4.

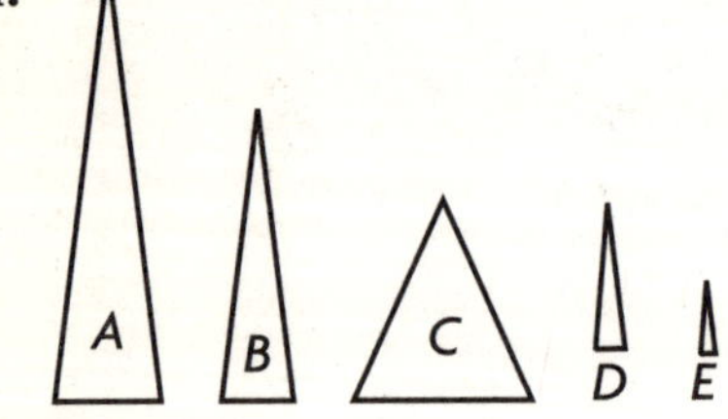

__________ **C**

5.

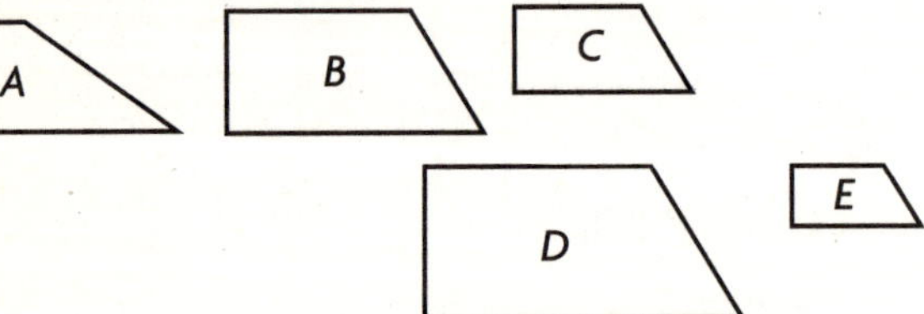

__________ **A**

6.

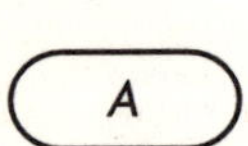

__________ **D**

Hidden Similarity

Use the fact that similar figures have corresponding sides with the same ratio to find all rectangles that are similar.

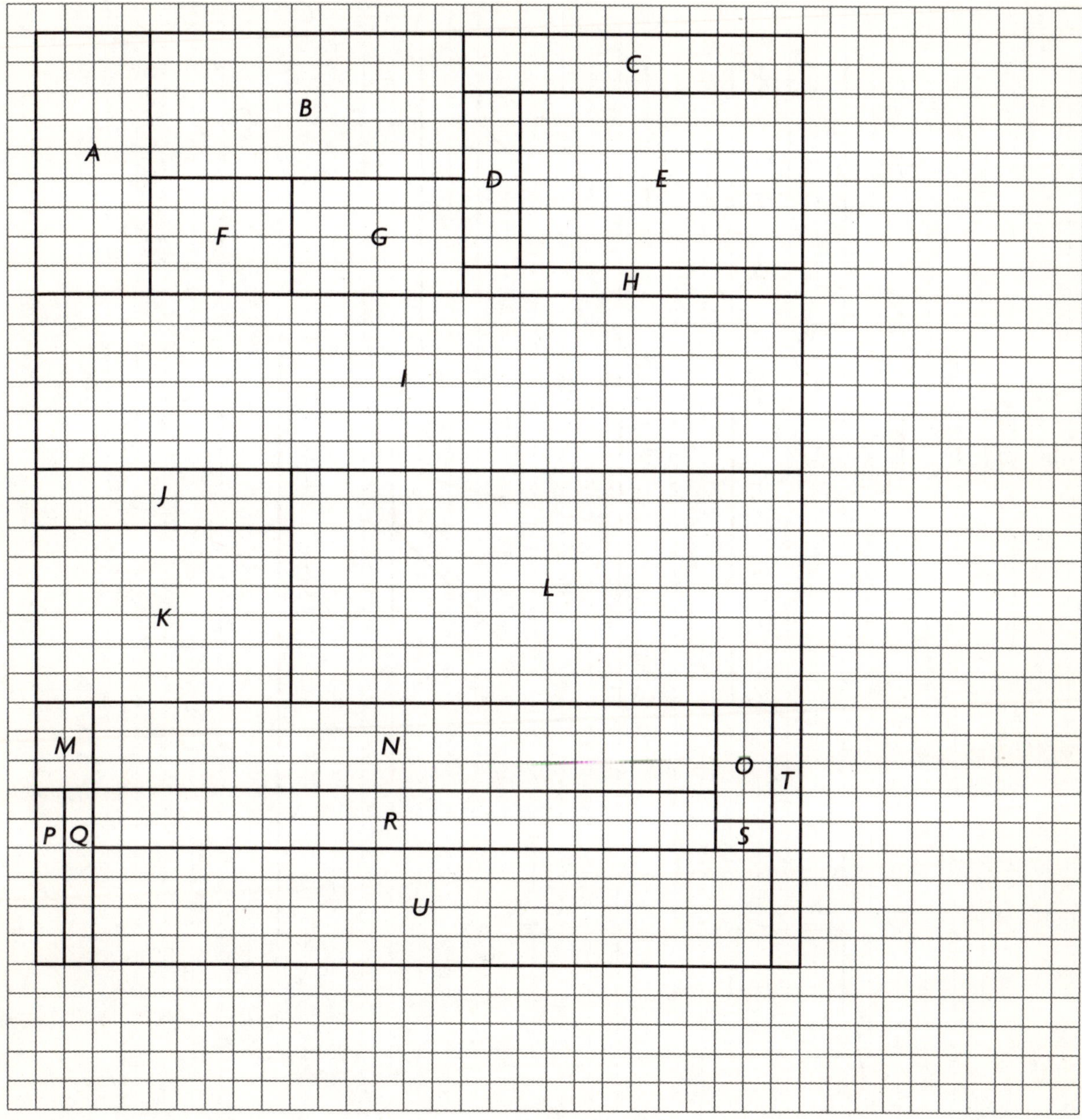

_A_ and _L_; _C_, _P_, _U_, and _Q_; _O_ and _S_; _G_, _K_, and _M_; _I_ and _J_

STRETCH YOUR THINKING E85

Enlargements

The drawing below is 15 by 10. Use proportions to enlarge it to 30 by 20 on the graph paper.

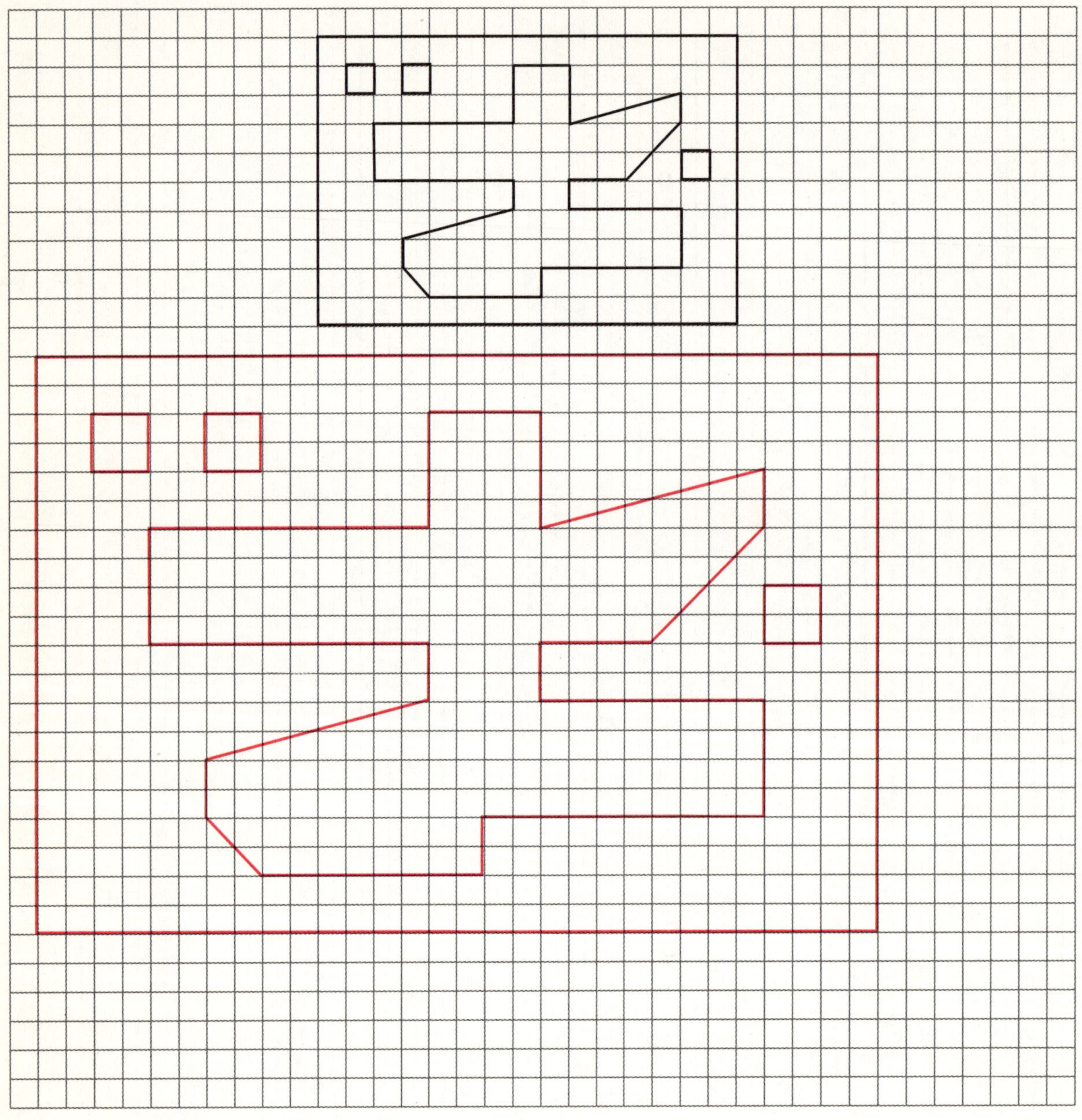

Line of Sight

At noon there are hardly any shadows to use indirect measurement.
Instead, you can measure in the following way.

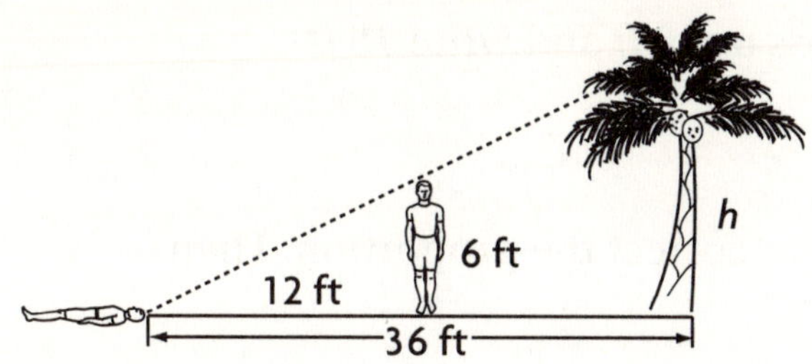

Lie on the ground, and line up the top of an object with the top of
another person's head. This creates two similar triangles. You can then
form the following proportion:

$$\frac{h}{6} = \frac{36}{12}$$
$$12 \times h = 6 \times 36$$
$$12h = 216$$
$$\frac{12h}{12} = \frac{216}{12}$$
$$h = 18$$

So, $h = 18$ ft.

Find the missing heights in each drawing. Round to the nearest foot.

1.

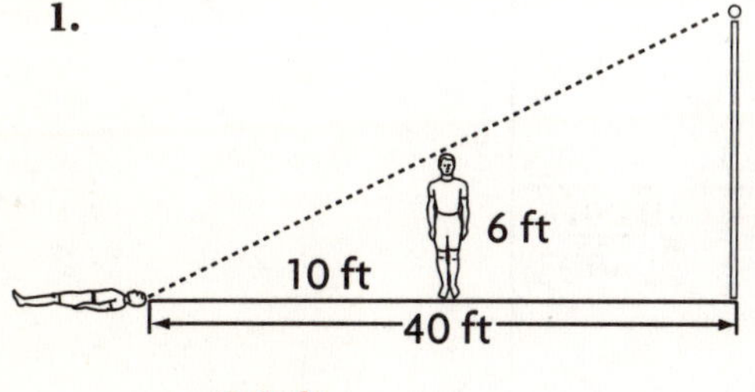

_____**24 ft**_____

2.

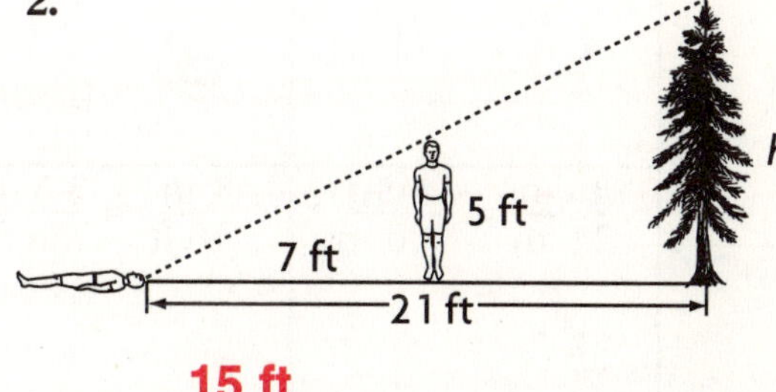

_____**15 ft**_____

3.

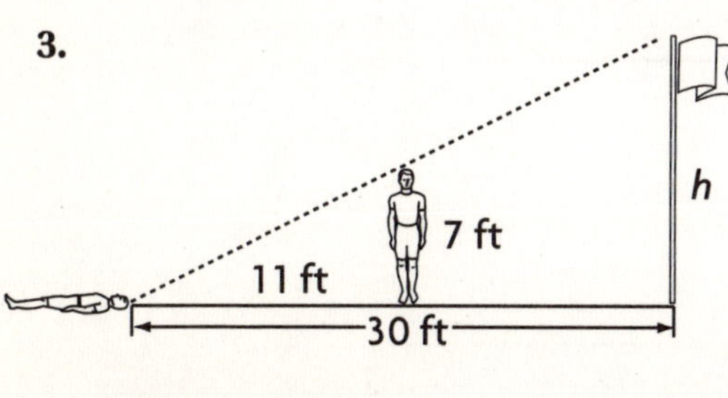

_____**about 19 ft**_____

4.

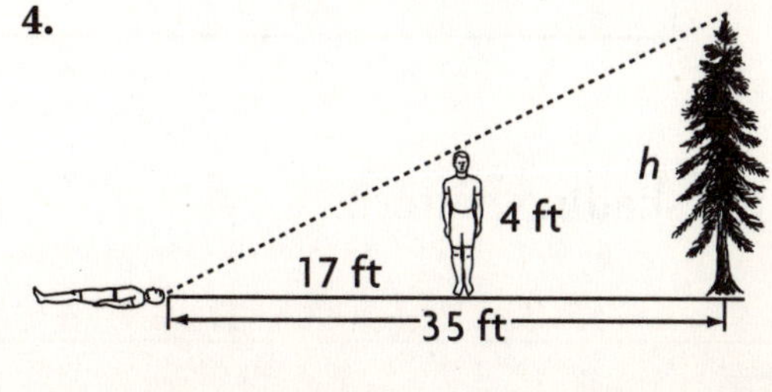

_____**about 8 ft**_____

STRETCH YOUR THINKING   E87

Shady Proportions

Some of the proportions in the rectangle below are correct and some
are not. Find the errors, and correct them by changing the *last term*.

For example, $\frac{1 \text{ in.}}{3 \text{ ft}} = \frac{6 \text{ in.}}{8 \text{ ft}}$ is wrong. So cross out *8 ft* and write *18 ft*

18 ft

to form the correct proportion.

Shade in all the squares where you had to correct the proportion. Then
describe the shading pattern.

$\frac{1 \text{ in.}}{4 \text{ ft}} = \frac{8 \text{ in.}}{32 \text{ ft}}$	$\frac{1 \text{ cm}}{3 \text{ m}} = \frac{5 \text{ cm}}{25 \text{ m}}$ **15 m**	$\frac{1 \text{ cm}}{20 \text{ km}} = \frac{7 \text{ cm}}{140 \text{ km}}$
$\frac{1 \text{ in.}}{8 \text{ ft}} = \frac{4 \text{ in.}}{32 \text{ in.}}$ **32 ft**	$\frac{1 \text{ in.}}{9 \text{ ft}} = \frac{10 \text{ in.}}{90 \text{ ft}}$	$\frac{4 \text{ cm}}{1 \text{ mm}} = \frac{2 \text{ cm}}{8 \text{ mm}}$ **0.5 mm**
$\frac{1 \text{ in.}}{2 \text{ ft}} = \frac{100 \text{ in.}}{200 \text{ ft}}$	$\frac{1 \text{ cm}}{12 \text{ m}} = \frac{8 \text{ cm}}{48 \text{ m}}$ **96 m**	$\frac{1 \text{ in.}}{20 \text{ yd}} = \frac{5 \text{ in.}}{100 \text{ yd}}$
$\frac{1 \text{ cm}}{2.5 \text{ m}} = \frac{4 \text{ cm}}{100 \text{ m}}$ **10 m**	$\frac{1 \text{ in.}}{16 \text{ ft}} = \frac{3.5 \text{ in.}}{56 \text{ ft}}$	$\frac{1 \text{ cm}}{3 \text{ m}} = \frac{10 \text{ cm}}{30 \text{ in.}}$ **30 m**

Describe the shading pattern.

__________ Alternate squares are shaded,

__________ creating a checkerboard pattern.

House Plans

The diagram gives the plans for the first floor of a new house. The plans are drawn using the scale 1 in. = 6 ft.

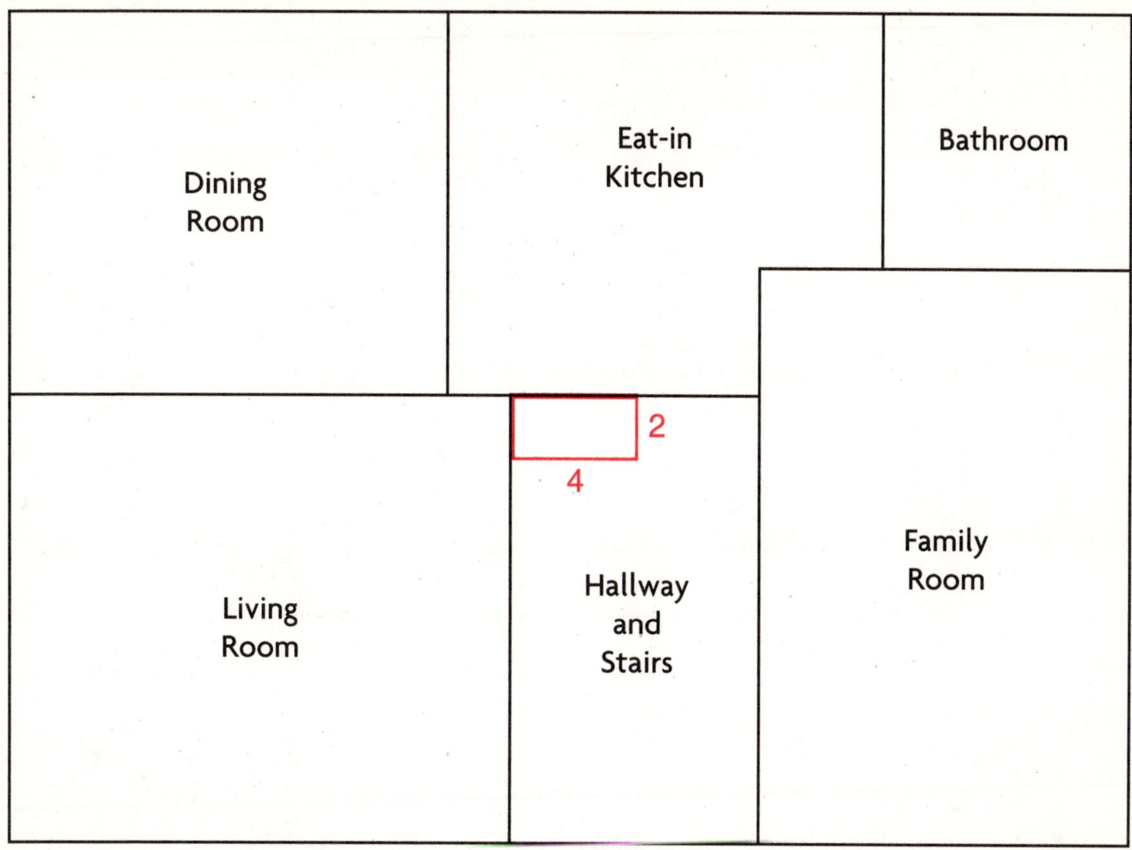

Measure each room. Then find the actual dimensions, to the nearest foot, for the following rooms.

1. Living room ______**16 ft × 14 ft**______

2. Family room ______**18 ft × 12 ft**______

3. Dining room ______**14 ft × 12 ft**______

4. Bathroom ______**8 ft × 8 ft**______

5. A closet is planned in the area marked "Hallway and Stairs." It will be 4 ft wide and 2 ft deep, and will be in the corner bordering the living room and kitchen. Draw the closet to scale on the diagram. **See figure above.**

6. Label all the dimensions, to the nearest foot, for the eat-in kitchen.

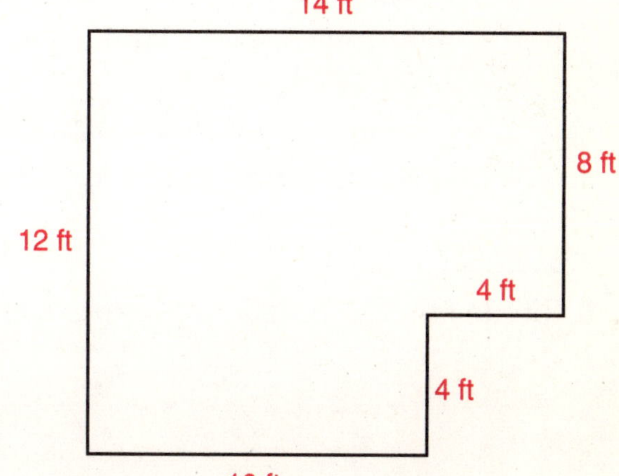

Go for the Globe

Madrid is due east of
New York. But no pilot
would fly due east to get
there. That is because a
great-circle route is shorter.

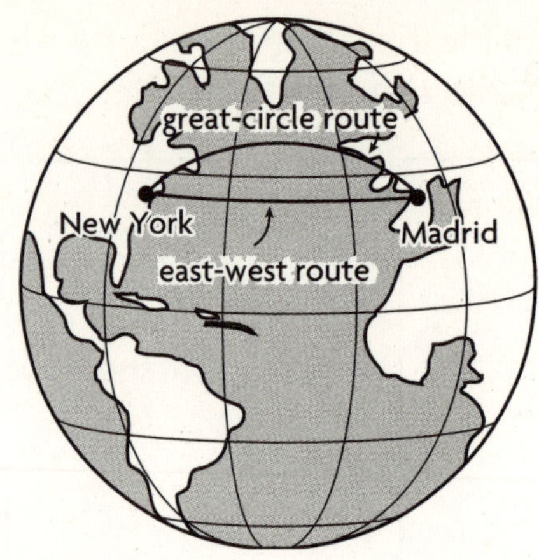

A great circle is a circle on a sphere with the same center as the sphere.
(Remember, east-west lines of latitude are not great circles, except for
the equator.)

Look at a globe. You wouldn't fly due west from Los Angeles to Tokyo.
The shortest route would take you near Alaska!

Estimate the great-circle route for each pair of cities. Then name
a country or major city near which the great-circle route
is located. **Possible answers are given.**

1. New Orleans to Cairo, Egypt

   Spain

2. Miami, Florida, to Bombay, India

   Poland

3. Mexico City to Tokyo

   Portland, OR

4. Rome, Italy, to Sydney, Australia

   Burma

5. Casablanca, Morocco, to Los Angeles

   Chicago

6. Rio de Janeiro, Brazil, to Montreal, Quebec

   Bermuda

The Golden Touch

The Golden Ratio is about 1.6 to 1. But the *exact* value is closer to 1.62 to 1. To find the exact value of the Golden Ratio, study this sequence of numbers.

The Fibonacci Sequence: 1, 1, 2, 3, 5, 8, 13, . . .

1. Explain how the next term is calculated.

Add the two previous terms.

2. The first seven terms are given. Name the next five terms.

21, 34, 55, 89, 144

Now it's time to get out your calculator.

3. Form the ratio of each term to the previous term in the Fibonacci Sequence. List the first 11 ratios in the sequence. The first three are given.

$$\frac{1}{1}, \frac{2}{1}, \frac{3}{2}, \frac{5}{3}, \frac{8}{5}, \frac{13}{8}, \frac{21}{13},$$

$$\frac{34}{21}, \frac{55}{34}, \frac{89}{55}, \frac{144}{89}$$

4. Using your calculator, write each ratio as a decimal to three decimal places.

1.000, 2.000, 1.500, 1.667, 1.600, 1.625, 1.615,

1.619, 1.618, 1.618, 1.618

The further you go with the ratios, the closer you get to the Golden Ratio.

5. To three decimal places, the value of the Golden Ratio is ___**1.618**___ .

6. Does your answer to Exercise 5 appear to be the *exact* value of the Golden Ratio? Explain.

No, but the ratios stay quite close to 1.618.

Measurement Puzzle

Across

1. 31 lb = ________?________ oz
2. 468 in. = ________?________ yd
3. 161 days = ________?________ weeks
4. 13 yd = ________?________ in.
5. 51 qt = ________?________ c
6. 21 weeks = ________?________ days
7. 12 qt = ________?________ fl oz
8. 129 gal = ________?________ qt
9. 45 weeks = ________?________ days
10. 53 qt = ________?________ c
11. 11 hr = ________?________ min
12. 12 qt = ________?________ pt
13. 117 yd = ________?________ ft
14. 6 T = ________?________ lb
15. 5 mi = ________?________ ft

Down

1. 18 days = ________?________ hr
4. 9 mi = ________?________ ft
11. 80 c = ________?________ fl oz
12. 29 weeks = ________?________ days
13. 62 c = ________?________ pt
14. $9\frac{1}{2}$ ft = ________?________ in.
16. 79 gal = ________?________ qt
17. 7 gal = ________?________ fl oz
18. 34 gal = ________?________ fl oz
19. 12 gal = ________?________ c
20. 50 pt = ________?________ qt
21. 12 lb = ________?________ oz

Math Tip Puzzle

Match each metric measurement in Column 1 with an equivalent measure in Column 2. Then write each corresponding letter on the lines below marked with the exercise number to discover the Math Tip.

Column 1

M	1.	17 kg
S	2.	25 mL
G	3.	500 dm
U	4.	200 cg
A	5.	615 cm
O	6.	170 dg
P	7.	0.25 L
W	8.	0.5 km
C	9.	20 g
N	10.	0.615 km
E	11.	1.7 g
H	12.	250 L
I	13.	5,000 m
R	14.	0.2 kg
T	15.	6,150 mm

Column 2

- (A) 6.15 m
- (C) 200 dg
- (E) 170 cg
- (G) 50 m
- (H) 2,500 dL
- (I) 5 km
- (M) 17,000 g
- (N) 615 m
- (O) 17 g
- (P) 250 mL
- (R) 2,000 dg
- (S) 0.025 L
- (T) 6.15 m
- (U) 2 g
- (W) 5,000 dm

W R I T E A
8   14   13   15   11   5

P R O P O R T I O N T O
7   14   6   7   6   14   15   13   6   10   15   6

C H A N G E M E T R I C
9   12   5   10   3   11   1   11   15   14   13   9

U N I T S
4   10   13   15   2

STRETCH YOUR THINKING   **E93**

The Sky Is Shrinking!

The table shows the total height America's tallest skyscrapers.
Use the table to answer the questions below.

AMERICA'S TALLEST SKYSCRAPERS		Height to Roof	
Name of Building	City	Feet	Meters
Sears Tower	Chicago	1,454	443
World Trade Center	New York City	1,350	411
Empire State Building	New York City	1,250	381
Amoco Building	Chicago	1,136	346
John Hancock Center	Chicago	1,127	344
First Interstate World Center	Los Angeles	1,018	310
Texas Commerce Tower	Houston	1,002	305

1. Which measurement is more precise, to the nearest foot or to the nearest meter? Explain.

   To the nearest foot; a foot is a smaller unit of measure.

2. What is the height of the First Interstate World Center to the nearest yard?

   $339\frac{1}{3}$ yd

3. Give the height of the World Trade Center in kilometers.

   0.411 km

4. What is the height of the Amoco Building in centimeters?

   34,600 cm

5. How many millimeters taller is the Sears Tower than the Texas Commerce Tower?

   138,000 mm

6. Which building listed in the table has a height of $375\frac{2}{3}$ yd?

   John Hancock Center

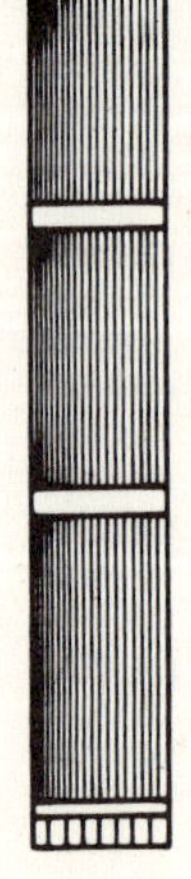
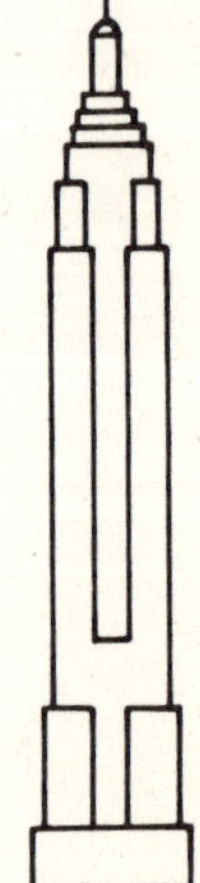

Vacation Plan

Angel's family is planning a trip to Texas. They want to visit the following locations: Austin, Dallas, Fort Worth, Houston, and San Antonio. Use the network below to identify the shortest route and also the longest route for Angel's family.

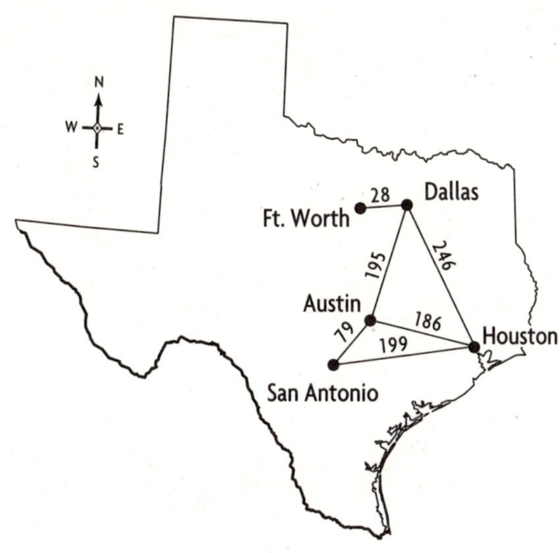

Shortest Route

Houston to San Antonio to

Austin to Dallas to Fort Worth;

501 mi

Longest Route

Fort Worth to Dallas to Houston

to San Antonio to Austin;

552 mi

Plan your own trip through Texas. List the cities you will visit and the total mileage of your trip.

Check students' trips.

Designing Figures

Use the information to design a figure with the given perimeter. Be sure
to label the length of each side of your figure. **Check students' drawings.**

1. A rectangle with a perimeter of 62 ft

2. A pentagon with a perimeter of 30 cm

3. An irregular figure with 7 sides and a perimeter of 78 m

4. A trapezoid with a perimeter of 45.2 mi

5. An octagon with a perimeter of 38.6 cm

6. An irregular figure with 6 sides and a perimeter of 99.3 ft

7. A pentagon with a perimeter of 87.5 m

8. A parallelogram with a perimeter of 84.2 ft

Surprising Areas

Use an atlas from the library to help you find each area in square miles. Then circle the continent, country, state, island, or body of water with the greater area.

1. Alaska, U.S. _____ 586,400 mi^2 _____ (Mediterranean Sea) _____ 967,000 mi^2

2. North America _____ 9,420,000 mi^2 _____ (Africa) _____ 11,685,000 mi^2

3. (South America) _____ 6,870,000 mi^2 _____ Arctic Ocean _____ 5,427,000 mi^2

4. Europe _____ 3,825,000 mi^2 _____ (Canada) _____ 3,851,809 mi^2

5. (Indian Ocean) _____ 28,371,000 mi^2 _____ Asia _____ 17,085,000 mi^2

6. United States _____ 3,675,633 mi^2 _____ (People's Republic of China) _____ 3,691,500 mi^2

7. (Brazil) _____ 3,286,487 mi^2 _____ Australia _____ 2,967,909 mi^2

8. World (land) _____ 57,280,000 mi^2 _____ (Pacific Ocean) _____ 63,855,000 mi^2

9. (Texas, U.S.) _____ 267,339 mi^2 _____ France _____ 210,039 mi^2

10. Hawai'i, U.S. _____ 6,424 mi^2 _____ (Sicily, Italy) _____ 9,926 mi^2

11. (Haiti) _____ 10,714 mi^2 _____ Lake Erie _____ 9,940 mi^2

12. (Kentucky, U.S.) _____ 40,395 mi^2 _____ South Korea _____ 38,004 mi^2

13. Portugal _____ 35,510 mi^2 _____ (New York, U.S.) _____ 49,576 mi^2

14. Taiwan _____ 13,885 mi^2 _____ (Lake Superior) _____ 31,820 mi^2

15. Galápagos Islands _____ 3,075 mi^2 _____ (Puerto Rico, U.S.) _____ 3,435 mi^2

16. Japan _____ 143,727 mi^2 _____ (Iraq) _____ 173,260 mi^2

17. (Mexico) _____ 761,604 mi^2 _____ Iran _____ 636,300 mi^2

Rectangle Treasures

Find the area of each rectangle. Write in the same box the letters of the
exercises having the same area.

a. $l = 12; w = 6$ __**72**__   **b.** $l = 32; w = 3$ __**96**__   **c.** $l = 36; w = 2$ __**72**__

d. $l = 125; w = 3$ __**375**__   **e.** $l = 48; w = 3$ __**144**__   **f.** $l = 25; w = 15$ __**375**__

g. $l = 18; w = 4$ __**72**__   **h.** $l = 24; w = 4$ __**96**__   **i.** $l = 18; w = 8$ __**144**__

j. $l = 12; w = 8$ __**96**__   **k.** $l = 36; w = 4$ __**144**__   **l.** $l = 75; w = 5$ __**375**__

m. $l = 9; w = 8$ __**72**__   **n.** $l = 16; w = 9$ __**144**__   **o.** $l = 16; w = 6$ __**96**__

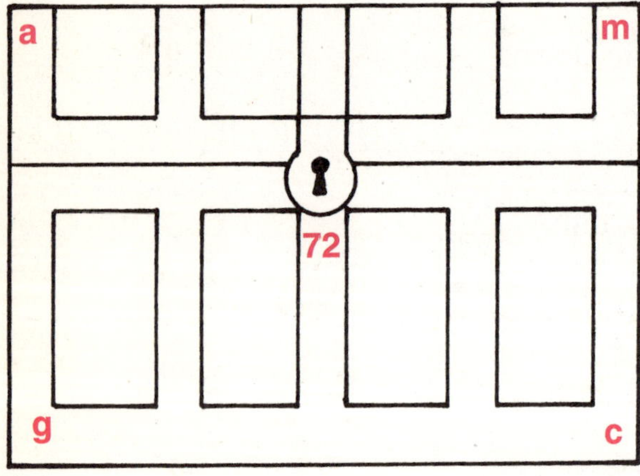

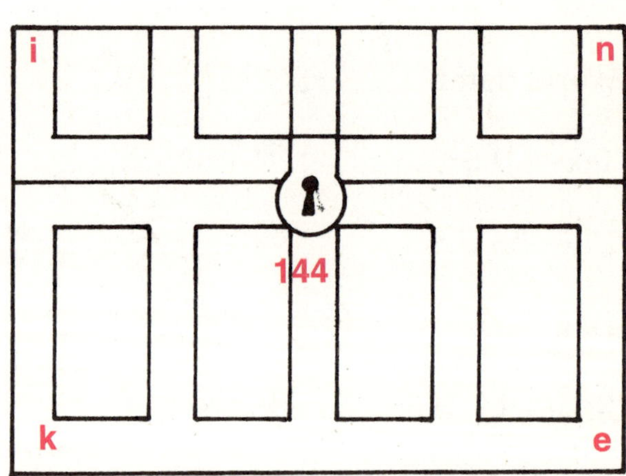

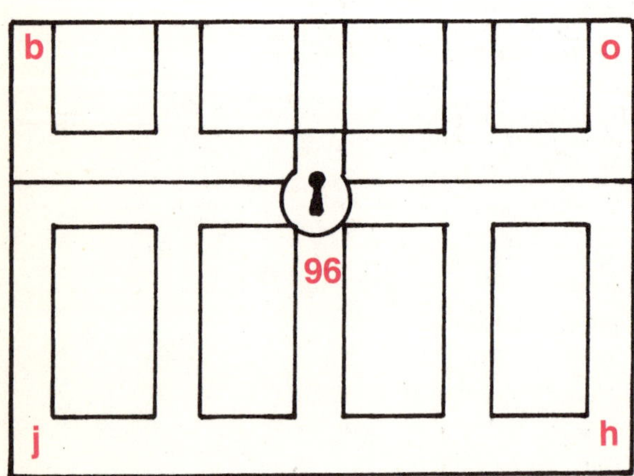

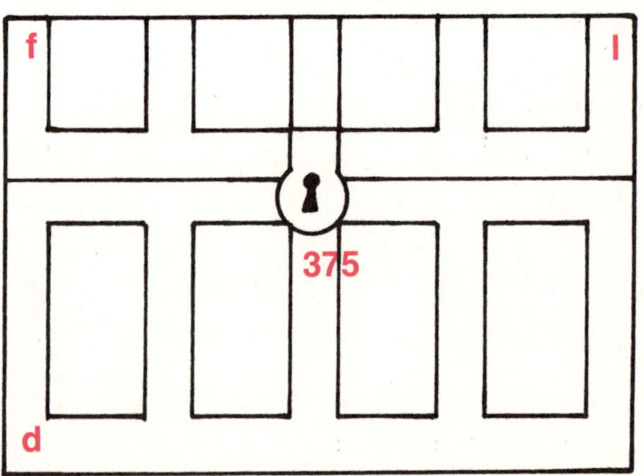

Perimeters and Presidents

N: 48	U: 32	M: 64	R: 25
R: 44	H: 43.5	A: 34	A: 78.75
S: 84	T: 24	Y: 42	R: 112

Match the perimeter and area of each figure with a number below.
Then write the letter of the answer choice above the exercise number
at the bottom of the page. You will write the name of the 33rd
President of the United States.

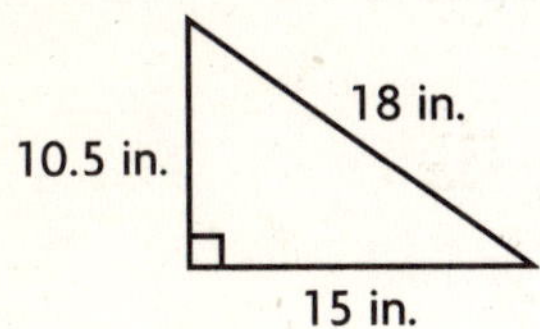

1. $P = $ __43.5__ in.

2. $A = $ __78.75__ in.^{2}

3. $P = $ __44__ cm

4. $A = $ __112__ cm^2

5. $P = $ __42__ ft

6. $A = $ __84__ ft^2

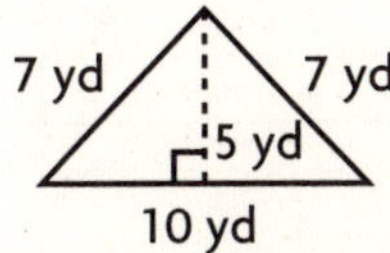

7. $P = $ __24__ yd

8. $A = $ __25__ yd^2

9. $P = $ __32__ m

10. $A = $ __64__ m^2

11. $P = $ __34__ yd

12. $A = $ __48__ yd^2

H	**A**	**R**	**R**	**Y**		**S**		**T**	**R**	**U**	**M**	**A**	**N**
1	2	3	4	5		6		7	8	9	10	11	12

A Better Buy

Which is the better buy? Explain. Write S for *same* if neither is a better buy. Then write the letter of your answer choice above the exercise number at the bottom of the page. You will write the name of a famous scientist who lived in the 19th century.

1. silk:

R 1.5 ft × 1 ft for $7.50

L 3 ft × 2 ft for $15.00

__L; $2.50 per ft^2 < $5.00 per ft^2__

2. artificial turf:

O 35 yd × 18 yd for $25,000

P 17.5 yd × 9 yd for $12,500

__O; $40 per yd^2 < $79 per yd^2__

3. murals:

P 3 ft × 8 ft for $240

U 6 ft × 16 ft for $720

__U; $7.50 per ft^2 < $10.00 per ft^2__

4. canvas:

I 3 yd × 4 yd for $120

L 1.5 yd × 2 yd for $42

__I; $10 per yd^2 < $14 per yd^2__

5. 8-in. × 11-in. paper:

A 100 sheets for $1.58

E 250 sheets for $3.95

__S__

6. carpet:

P 9 ft × 15 ft for $270

I 18 ft × 15 ft for $1,080

__P; $2 per ft^2 < $4 per ft^2__

7. canvas:

A 2.5 yd × 3.5 yd for $115.50

T 5 yd × 7 yd for $490.00

__A; $13.20 per yd^2 < $14.00 per yd^2__

8. grass seed for yard:

L 300 ft × 500 ft for $16

P 600 ft × 1,000 ft for $64

__S__

9. carpet:

A 6 ft × 7.5 ft for $540

T 12 ft × 15 ft for $1,080

__T; $6 per ft^2 < $12 per ft^2__

10. wrapping paper:

U 1.5 ft × 0.75 ft for $0.50

E 3 ft × 1.5 ft for $1.00

__E; $0.22 per ft^2 < $0.44 per ft^2__

11. fabric:

U 12 ft × 3 ft for $39.60

L 6 ft × 4.5 ft for $32.40

__U; $1.10 per ft^2 < $1.20 per ft^2__

12. building lot:

R 50 ft × 50 ft for $50,000

T 25 ft × 25 ft for $25,000

__R; $20 per ft^2 < $40 per ft^2__

__L__ __O__ __U__ __I__ __S__   __P__ __A__ __S__ __T__ __E__ __U__ __R__
 1   2   3   4   5   6   7   8   9   10   11   12

Find the Radius

If you know the area of a circle, you can use a calculator to find the radius.

The area of the top of a snare drum is 314 in.^{2}

$A = 314$ in.$^2 = \pi r^2$

Divide by π to find r^2.   314 ÷ 3.14 = | 100 |

Use the square root key.   √ | 10 |

The radius of the snare drum is 10 in.

Use a calculator to find the radius.

1. The area of a circular glass window is 3.14 yd^2. $r = 1$ yd

2. The area of a circular swimming pool is 706.5 ft^2. $r = 15$ ft

3. The area of a circular tabletop is 28.26 ft^2. $r = 3$ ft

4. The area of a large pizza is 153.86 in.^{2} $r = 7$ in.

5. The area of a dartboard is 1,256 in.^{2} $r = 20$ in.

6. The area of a quarter is 4.5216 cm^2. $r = 1.2$ cm

7. The area of a small pizza is 78.5 in.^{2} $r = 5$ in.

8. The area of the top of a circular cake is 254.34 in.^{2} $r = 9$ in.

9. The area of a circular flower garden is 50.24 ft^2. $r = 4$ ft

10. The area of a circular top of a water tank is 1,962.5 ft^2. $r = 25$ ft

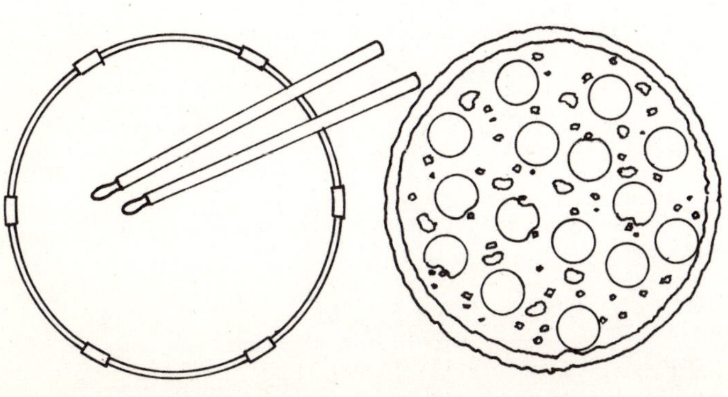

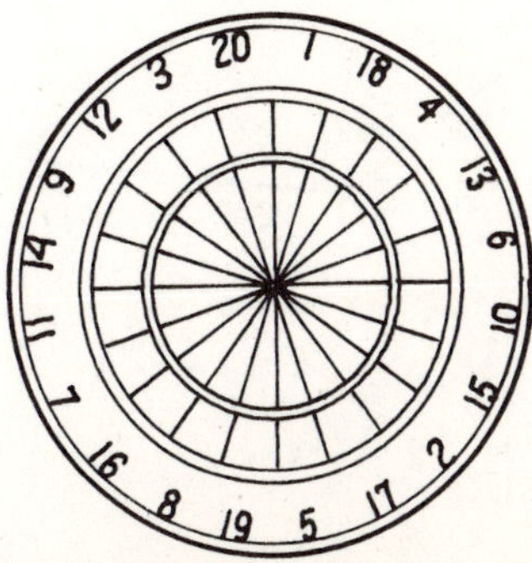

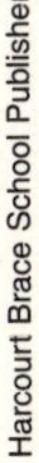

Compound Volumes

Find the volume of each figure.

1.

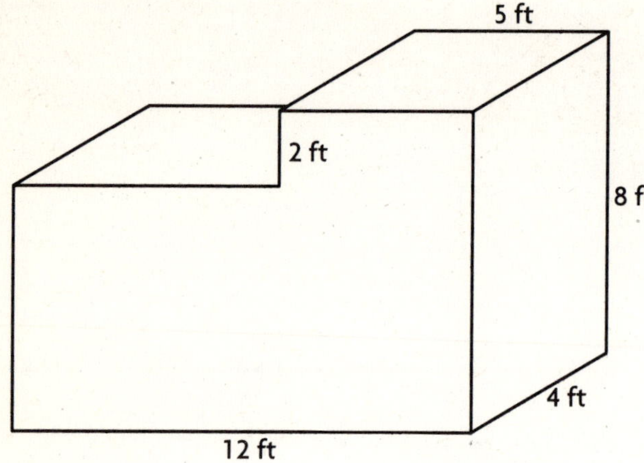

___________________ **328 ft³**

2.

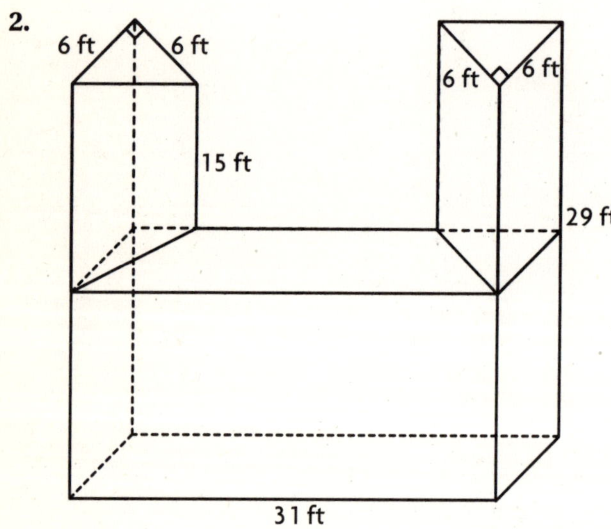

___________________ **3,144 ft³**

3.

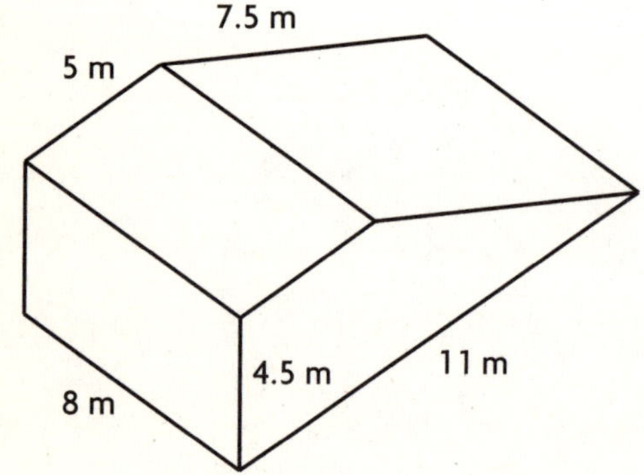

___________________ **288 m³**

After Doubling?

When you double all the dimensions of a rectangular prism, the volume is increased by a factor of 8.

What happens when you triple or quadruple the dimensions of a rectangular prism?

Complete each table.

1.

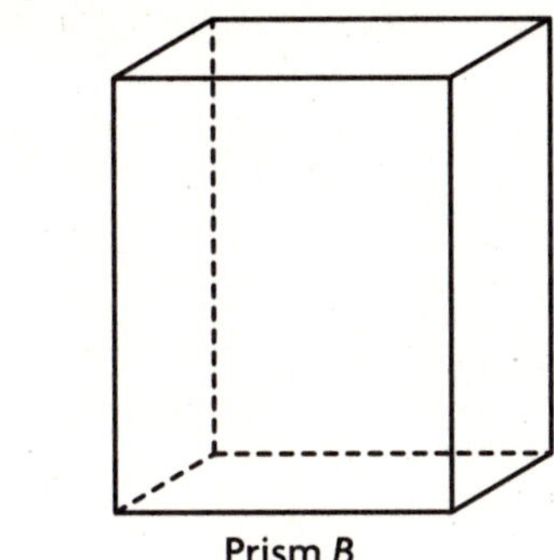

	Length	Width	Height	Volume
Prism A	3 cm	2 cm	4 cm	24 cm³
Prism B	9 cm	6 cm	12 cm	648 cm³
Ratio: $\frac{B}{A}$	$\frac{9}{3}$, or 3	$\frac{6}{2}$, or 3	$\frac{12}{4}$, or 3	$\frac{648}{24}$, or 27

2.

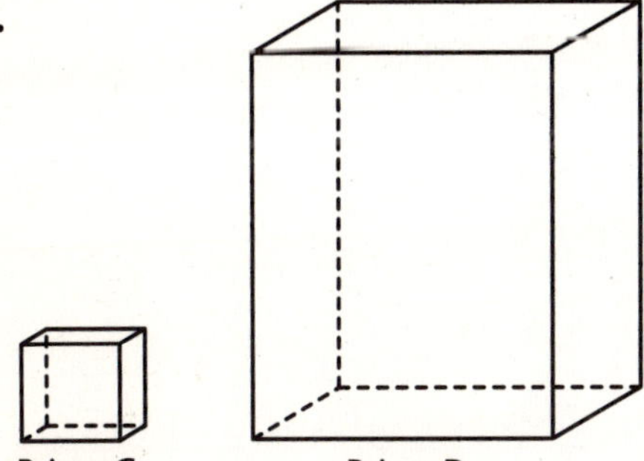

	Length	Width	Height	Volume
Prism C	3 cm	2 cm	4 cm	24 cm³
Prism D	12 cm	8 cm	16 cm	1,536 cm³
Ratio: $\frac{D}{C}$	$\frac{12}{3}$, or 4	$\frac{8}{2}$, or 4	$\frac{16}{4}$, or 4	$\frac{1,536}{24}$, or 64

STRETCH YOUR THINKING   E103

What's Left?

Each cylinder has a hole or holes cut through it. Find the volume that is
left. Round to the nearest whole number.

1.

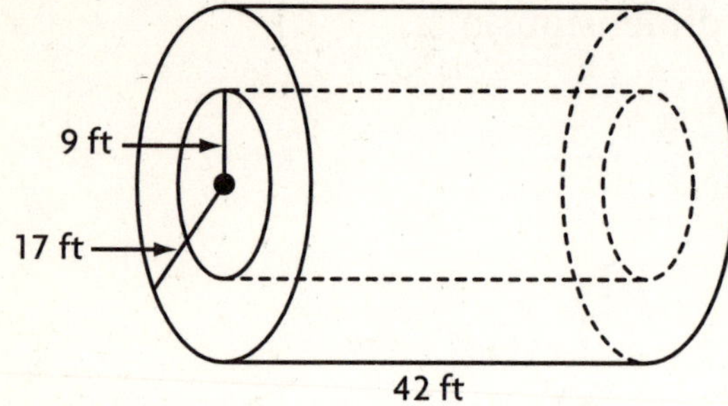

_____________________ **about 27,431 ft³**

2.

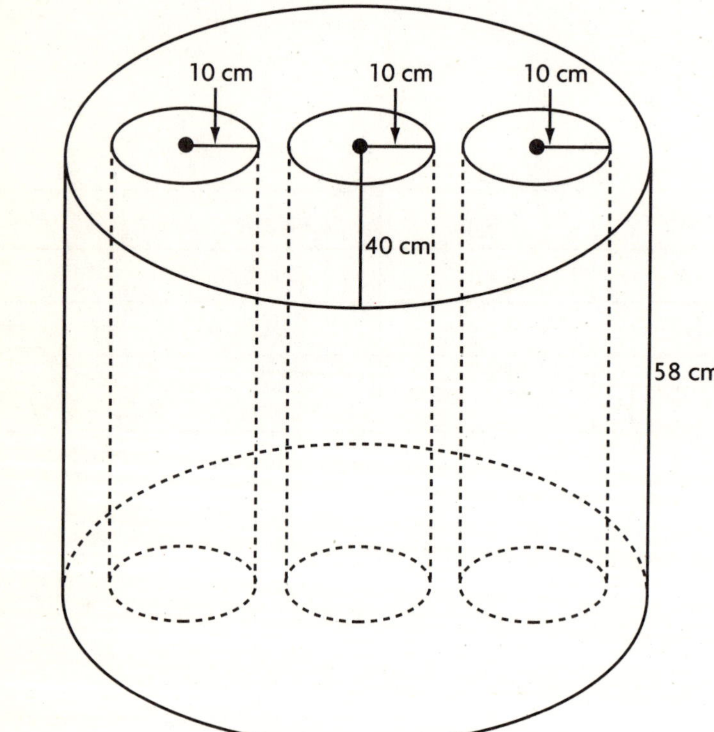

_____________________ **about 236,756 cm³**

3.

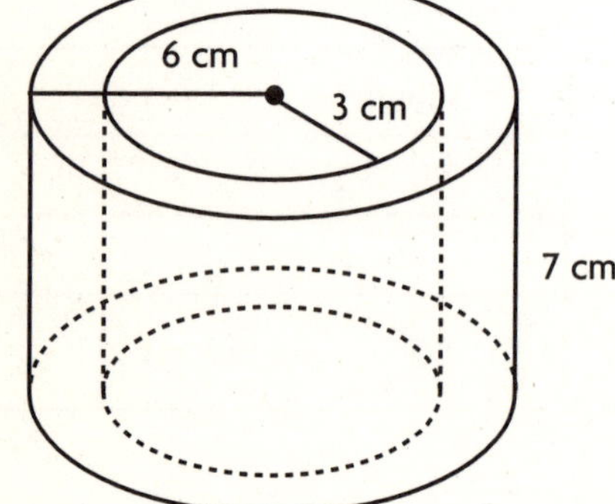

_____________________ **about 593 cm³**

E104 STRETCH YOUR THINKING

Cover That Building!

The Davidsons want to paint the outside of their barn. The number of
doors and windows are the same on opposite sides of the barn. They
plan on painting the doors green, the four walls blue, the peaks in
front and back yellow, and the roof red. The paint costs $15.87 a
gallon. A gallon of paint will cover 345 square feet. How many gallons
of each color do they need to buy? How much will it cost them to
paint the barn?

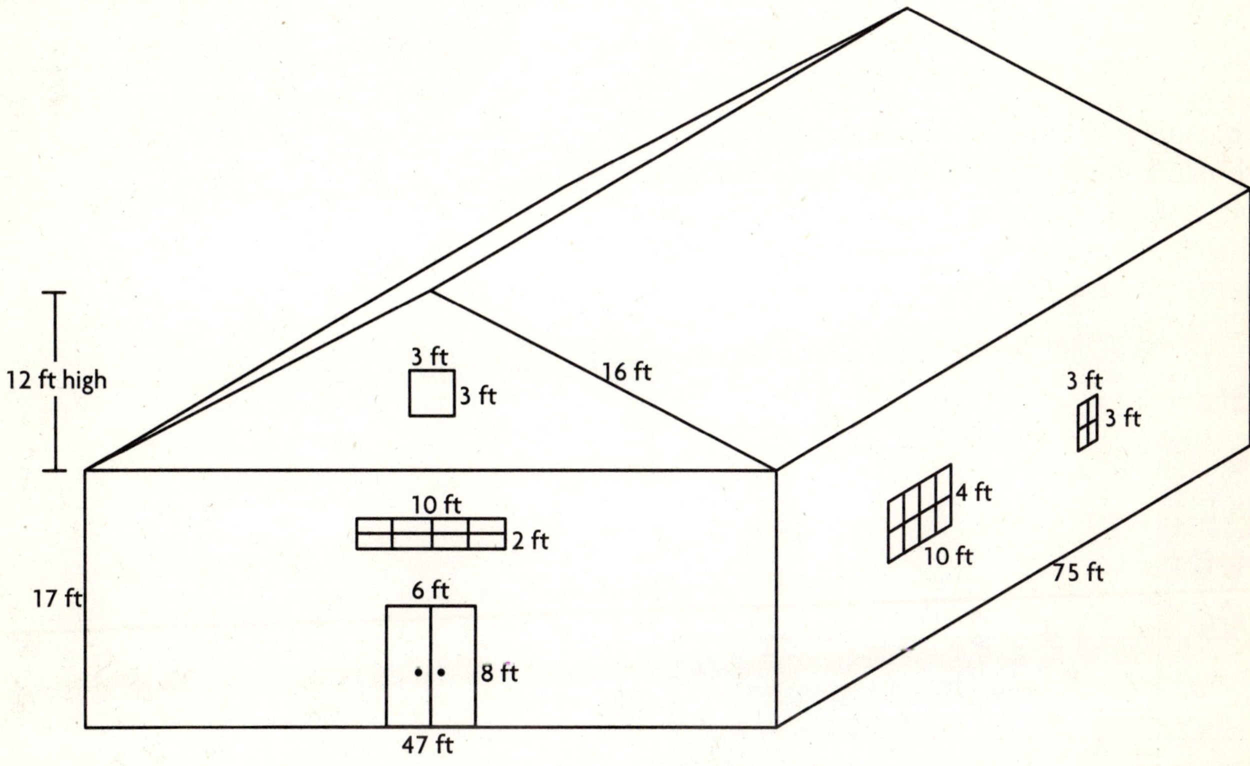

1 gallon of green paint, 7 gallons of red paint,

2 gallons of yellow paint, 12 gallons of blue paint;

total cost: $349.14

Never-Ending Game

This game can be played by one to four players. Everyone takes turns spinning the pointer and moving their game piece along the board. Positive numbers move forward and negative numbers move backward. You cannot go farther back than START. The object is to be the first to reach the end or to go past it.

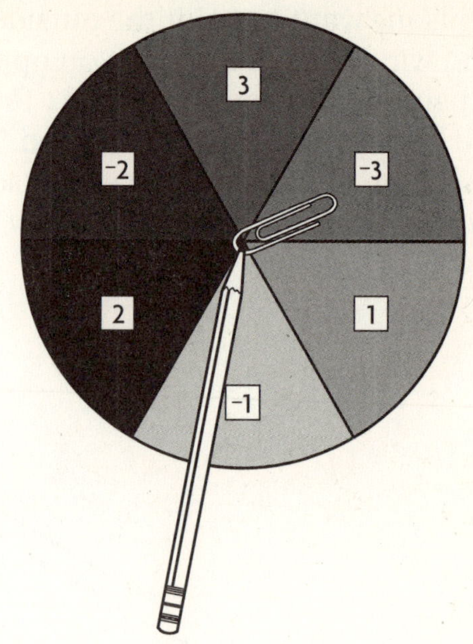

To use the spinner, use a paper clip as shown and center it on the circle. Hold it in place using the tip of a pencil, and then spin the clip. Use different coins or counters for game pieces.

Start

Finish

What Am I?

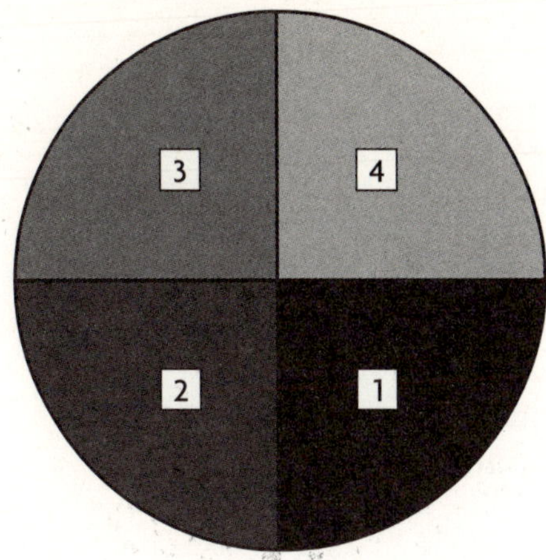

Spinner A

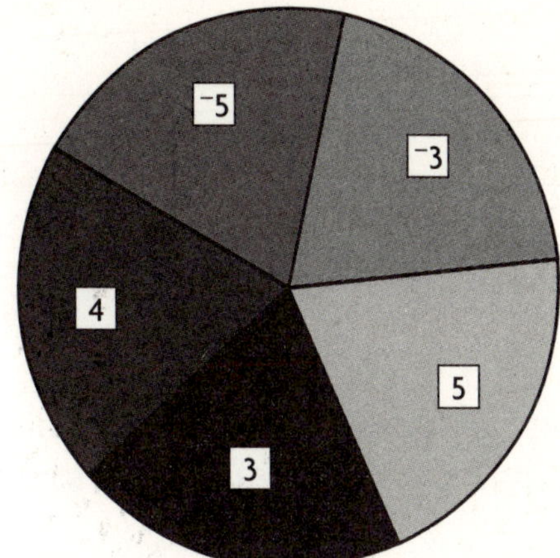

Spinner B

This game is for two people.

Use a paper clip and a pencil for the spinner.

- Each player will spin each pointer once.
- Form a number using the number from Spinner A as the numerator and the number from Spinner B as the denominator.
- Write the number in the Venn diagram in any category you want. Once you place a number in the diagram, it cannot be changed.
- The first player to get two numbers in each category is the winner.

Rational Numbers

Integers

Whole Numbers

Forever

Use a calculator to find the pattern in the following repeating decimals.

1. $\frac{1}{7}$

_____0.142857_____

2. $\frac{2}{7}$

_____0.285714_____

3. $\frac{3}{7}$

_____0.428571_____

4. $\frac{4}{7}$

_____0.571428_____

5. $\frac{5}{7}$

_____0.714285_____

6. $\frac{6}{7}$

_____0.857142_____

Sometimes a calculator does not give enough decimal places to see the pattern. In these cases you may have to divide using paper and pencil.

Find the terminating or repeating decimal for each number.

7. $\frac{1}{2}$

_____0.5_____

8. $\frac{1}{3}$

_____0.333333_____

9. $\frac{1}{4}$

_____0.25_____

10. $\frac{1}{5}$

_____0.2_____

11. $\frac{1}{7}$

_____0.142857_____

12. $\frac{1}{10}$

_____0.1_____

13. $\frac{1}{6}$

_____0.166666_____

14. $\frac{1}{8}$

_____0.125_____

15. $\frac{1}{9}$

_____0.1111111_____

16. $\frac{1}{11}$

_____0.090909_____

17. $\frac{1}{12}$

_____0.083333_____

18. $\frac{1}{13}$

_____0.076923_____

19. $\frac{1}{14}$

_____0.0714285_____

20. $\frac{1}{15}$

_____0.066666_____

21. $\frac{1}{16}$

_____0.0625_____

22. $\frac{1}{17}$

_____0.058823_____

23. $\frac{1}{18}$

_____0.055555_____

24. $\frac{1}{19}$

_____0.052631_____

25. $\frac{2}{3}$

_____0.6666666_____

26. $\frac{9}{11}$

_____0.818181_____

27. $\frac{7}{8}$

_____0.875_____

28. $\frac{3}{7}$

_____0.4285714_____

29. $\frac{7}{15}$

_____0.4666666_____

30. $\frac{2}{5}$

_____0.4_____

Math Pun

Find the numbers in the Math Pun that are between the pairs of
numbers in the list below. Then write the letter for the pair of numbers
above the number between them to discover the Math Pun.

S   2.7 and 2.9

L $\frac{3}{5}$ and 0.8

G $^-2.5$ and $^-1.3$

B $2\frac{1}{4}$ and 2.5

I $^-1\frac{1}{2}$ and $^-0.5$

R $\frac{2}{3}$ and $\frac{3}{4}$

U $1\frac{1}{3}$ and 1.4

H $\frac{1}{8}$ and $\frac{1}{4}$

O $^-3.4$ and $^-3.5$

A $\frac{1}{5}$ and 0.3

M $\frac{5}{6}$ and $\frac{7}{8}$

T $1\frac{1}{8}$ and 1.6

E $^-3.8$ and $^-3.9$

N   0 and $\frac{^-1}{8}$

K   2.53 and 2.43

MATH PUN:

R	A	T	I	O	N	A	L
$\frac{17}{24}$	$\frac{1}{4}$	1.25	$^-1$	$^-3.46$	$\frac{^-1}{16}$	$\frac{1}{4}$	0.7

N	U	M	B	E	R	S
$\frac{^-1}{16}$	1.35	$\frac{41}{48}$	2.4	$^-3.82$	$\frac{17}{24}$	2.8

T	H	I	N	K
1.25	$\frac{3}{16}$	$^-1$	$\frac{^-1}{16}$	2.5

S	T	R	A	I	G	H	T
2.8	1.25	$\frac{17}{24}$	$\frac{1}{4}$	$^-1$	$^-1.8$	$\frac{3}{16}$	1.25

And the Number Is?

Between any two numbers is always another number.

Place the following numbers along the path so that they get greater as you go along.

⁻1, 0.478, 1.908, 1.638, ⁻0.7, 1.50, 0.534, 1.999, 1.61, ⁻0.62, 1.53, 1.732, 1.64, ⁻0.07, 1.101, ⁻0.32, 1.7, 0, 0.24, 1.887, 0.3, 1.32, 0.52, ⁻0.92, 0.562, 1.642, 0.6, ⁻0.675, 0.234, ⁻0.234, 0.675, 1.01, 1.683, 1.236, ⁻0.001, 1.3, 1.854, ⁻0.9, 1.62, ⁻0.683, 0.62, ⁻0.11, 1.69, 1.1, 1.714, 1.28, 1.86, 1.903, 0.478, 1.4, 1.45, 0.78, 2

⁻1										
⁻0.92								1.1	1.101	1.236
⁻0.9	0	0.234	0.24	0.3				1.01		1.28
⁻0.7	⁻0.001			0.478				0.78		1.3
⁻0.683	⁻0.07			0.52	0.534	0.562	0.6	0.62	0.675	1.32
⁻0.675	⁻0.11									1.4
⁻0.62	⁻0.32	⁻0.234								1.45

1.683	1.642	1.64	1.638	1.62	1.61	1.53	1.50
1.69							
1.7							
1.714	1.732	1.854	1.86	1.887	1.903	1.908	1.999

2

Sum It Up

The integer at the top of each rectangle is the sum of four addends contained in the rectangle. Shade the boxes containing the addends you use to get the sum. You will use one addend in each row.

1.

⁻2	
+3	0
⁻9	**+1**
+10	⁻7
⁻16	⁻4

2.

+5	
+9	**+6**
⁻5	**⁻7**
⁻1	**⁻6**
+12	0

3.

⁻4	
⁻3	0
⁻8	⁻2
+10	**⁻6**
+3	**+13**

4.

+6	
+5	**+4**
0	**+12**
+6	**⁻9**
+4	**⁻1**

5.

⁻3	
+6	**⁻2**
⁻7	**0**
⁻9	+8
+8	+2

6.

0	
+10	**⁻6**
⁻2	+12
⁻6	⁻5
⁻9	**+14**

7.

+2	
+1	**⁻4**
+4	**⁻3**
+9	+2
⁻6	**0**

8.

⁻8	
⁻7	+2
⁻1	⁻5
⁻2	**⁻4**
+9	**+4**

9.

+4	
+5	⁻8
⁻3	**⁻6**
⁻2	+9
+7	⁻10

Create the Problem

Create a word problem that can be solved with each subtraction problem below. Then trade problems with a classmate, and solve each other's problems. **Check students' problems.**

1. $^-12 - {}^+7 =$ **$^-19$**

2. $^+15 - {}^-9 =$ **$^+24$**

3. $^-25 - {}^-17 =$ **$^-8$**

4. $^-32 - {}^+14 =$ **$^-46$**

5. $^-55 - {}^-23 =$ **$^-32$**

6. $^+78 - {}^-19 =$ **$^+97$**

Multiplication Tip

Match each product in Column 2 with its factors in Column 1. Write the corresponding letter on the line marked with the exercise number to discover the Math Tip.

Column 1		**Column 2**
F	1. $^-8 \times {}^-7$	A. $^-28$
R	2. $^+12 \times {}^-4$	C. $^+51$
I	3. $^+13 \times {}^+3$	D. $^+48$
A	4. $^-7 \times {}^+4$	E. $^-90$
O	5. $^-15 \times {}^-3$	F. $^+56$
D	6. $^-8 \times {}^-6$	G. $^-45$
T	7. $^-14 \times {}^-2$	H. $^+100$
G	8. $^+9 \times {}^-5$	I. $^+39$
V	9. $^-4 \times {}^+14$	N. $^-72$
C	10. $^-17 \times {}^-3$	O. $^+45$
P	11. $^-25 \times {}^+4$	P. $^-100$
E	12. $^+18 \times {}^-5$	R. $^-48$
U	13. $^-9 \times {}^-8$	S. $^-36$
S	14. $^-6 \times {}^+6$	T. $^+28$
W	15. $^-10 \times {}^-9$	U. $^+72$
N	16. $^-4 \times {}^+18$	V. $^-56$
H	17. $^-20 \times {}^-5$	W. $^+90$

T H E   P R O D U C T   O F
7 17 12   11   2   5   6   13   10   7   5   1

T W O   N E G A T I V E
7 15   5   16 12   8   4   7   3   9   12

I N T E G E R S   I S   A
3 16   7 12   8 12   2 14   3 14   4

P O S I T I V E   I N T E G E R
11   5 14   3   7   3   9 12   3 16   7 12   8 12   2

STRETCH YOUR THINKING   E113

Different Names for Numbers

Write an expression for each integer using any of the operations with integers and the integers $^{+}4$, $^{+}4$, $^{-}4$, and $^{-}4$. An example for Exercise 1 is done for you. **Possible answers are given.**

1. $^{-}2$ $(^{-}4 \div {}^{+}4) + (^{-}4 \div {}^{+}4)$

2. 0 $^{-}4 + {}^{+}4 + {}^{-}4 + {}^{+}4$

3. $^{-}1$ $(^{-}4 - {}^{+}4) \div (^{+}4 - {}^{-}4)$

4. 8 $(^{+}4 - {}^{-}4) + (^{-}4 + {}^{+}4)$

5. 24 $(^{-}4 \times {}^{-}4) + (^{+}4 + {}^{+}4)$

6. 15 $(^{-}4 \times {}^{-}4) - (^{+}4 \div {}^{+}4)$

7. $^{-}64$ $(^{-}4 - {}^{+}4) \times (^{+}4 - {}^{-}4)$

8. 2 $(^{-}4 \times {}^{-}4) \div (^{+}4 + {}^{+}4)$

9. 256 $(^{-}4 \times {}^{+}4) \times (^{-}4 \times {}^{+}4)$

10. 16 $(^{-}4 - {}^{-}4) + (^{+}4 \times {}^{+}4)$

11. 1 $(^{+}4 \times {}^{-}4) \div (^{+}4 \times {}^{-}4)$

12. $^{-}16$ $(^{+}4 \times {}^{-}4) + (^{-}4 + {}^{+}4)$

Which Letter?

To find the secret message, evaluate each algebraic expression to find the letter that matches the number under each line in the center. Evaluate each expression for $x = 6$.

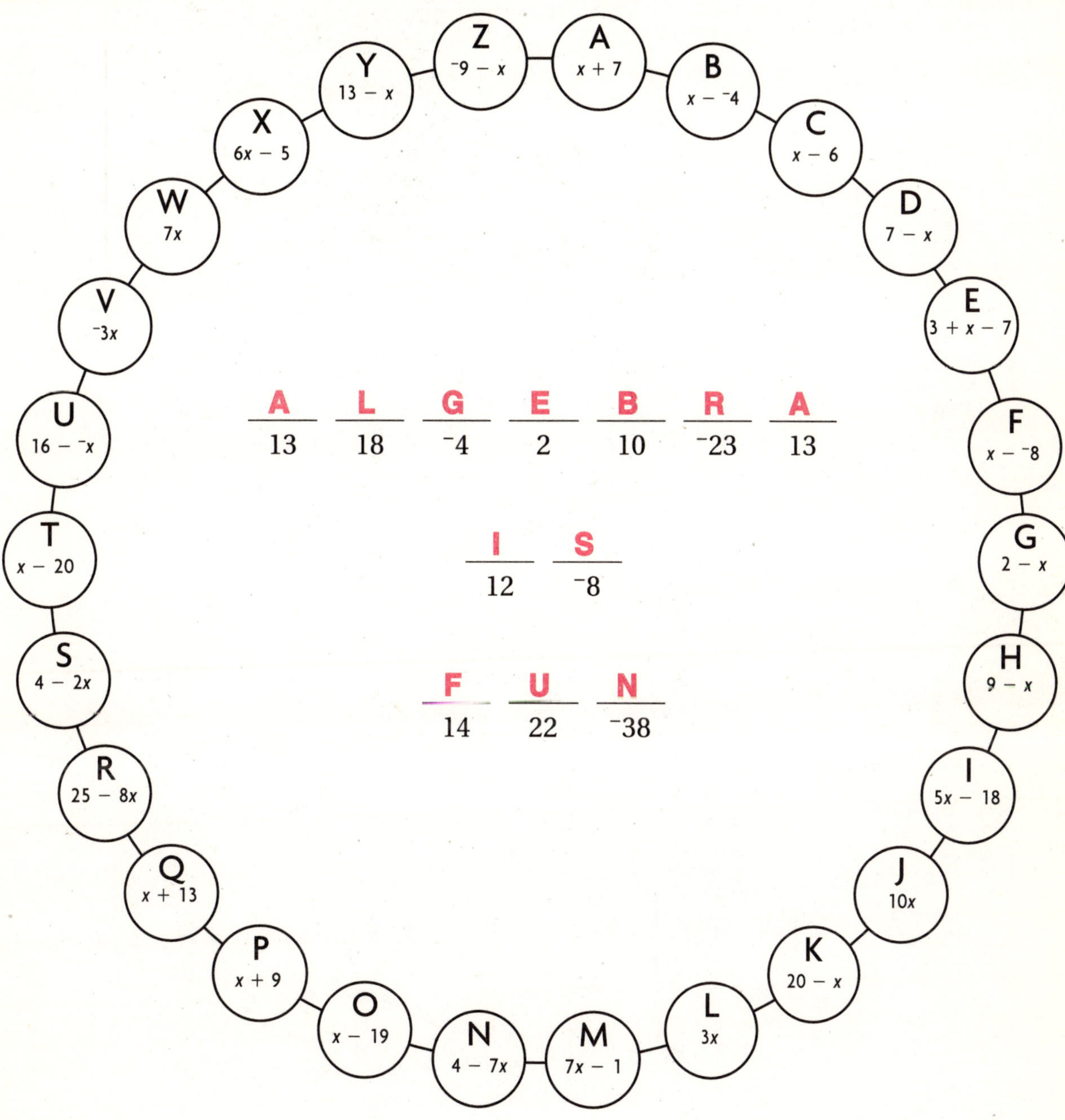

A L G E B R A
13 18 $^-4$ 2 10 $^-23$ 13

I S
12 $^-8$

F U N
14 22 $^-38$

STRETCH YOUR THINKING E115

Object Solving

In each figure, find what is needed to balance the last scale. **Possible answers are given.**

1.

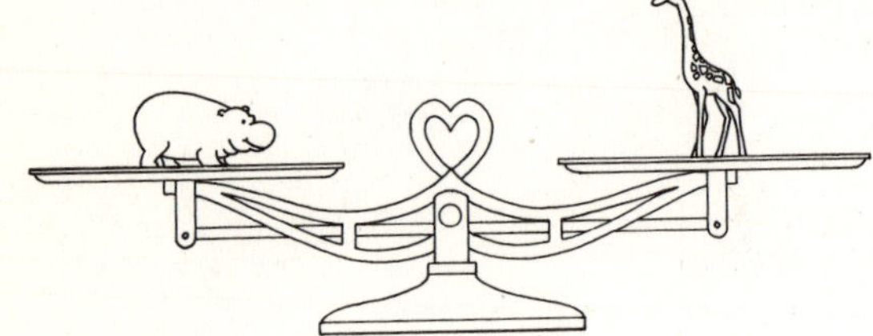

2.

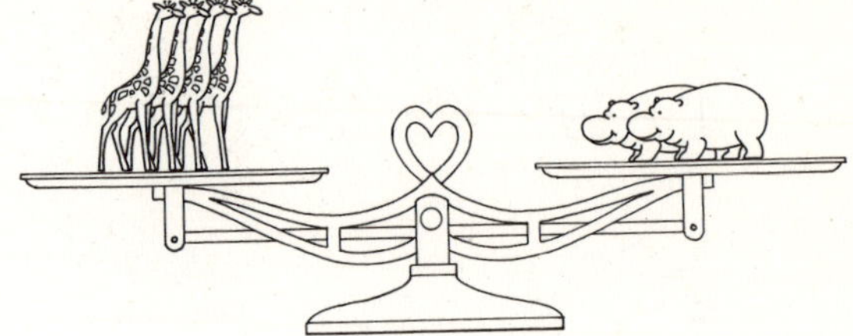

_______ **6 hippos or 6 giraffes** _______

_______ **2 hippos or 4 giraffes** _______

3.

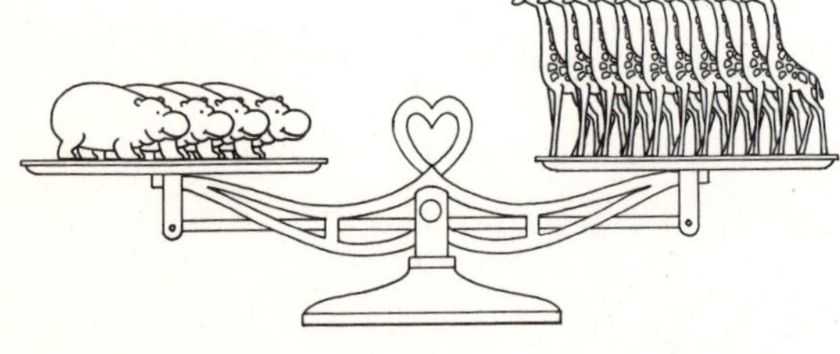

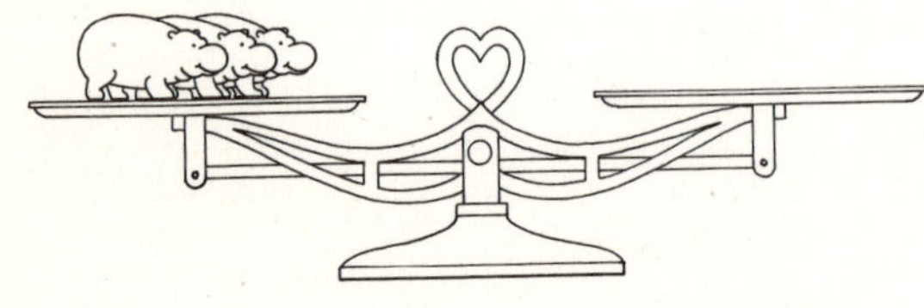

4.

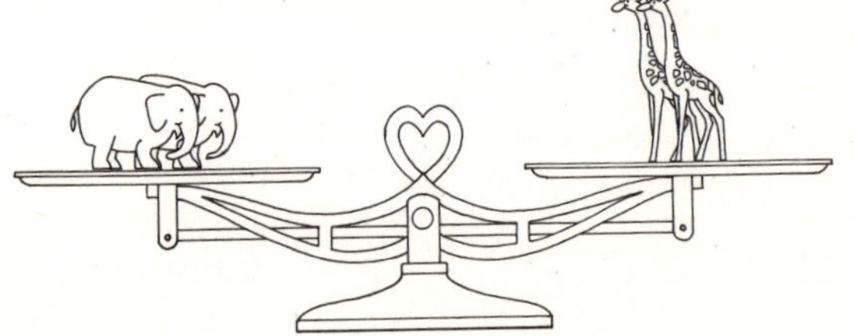

_______ **3 elephants or 7.5 giraffes** _______

_______ **4 elephants or 4 giraffes** _______

E116   STRETCH YOUR THINKING

Which Is Heaviest?

List the items on the scales from lightest to heaviest.

1.  

rectangular box, cylinder,

triangular box

2. 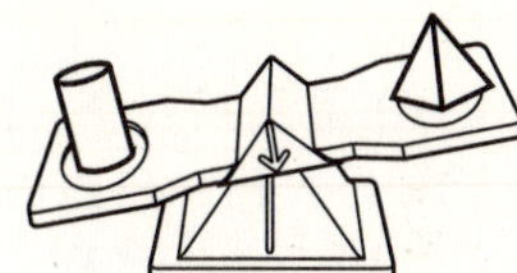

rectangular box, triangular box,

cylinder

3. 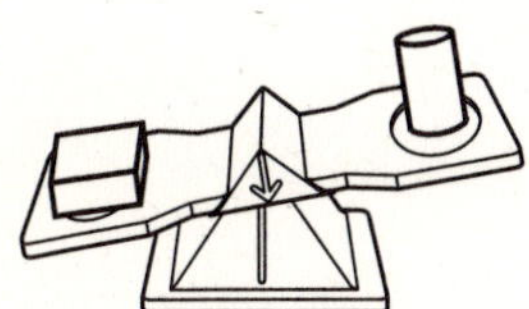

cylinder, rectangular box,

triangular box

4. 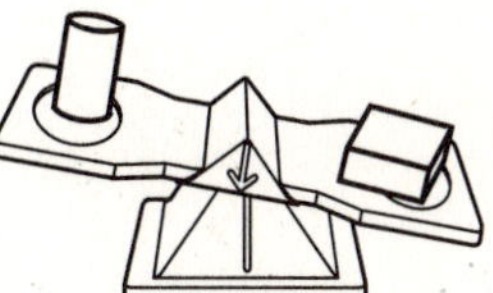 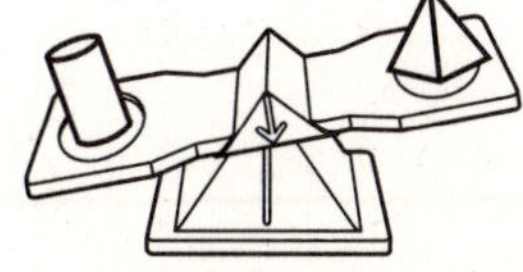

triangular box, cylinder,

rectangular box

5.  

cylinder, triangular box,

rectangular box

6. 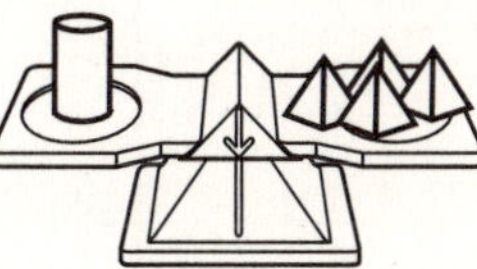 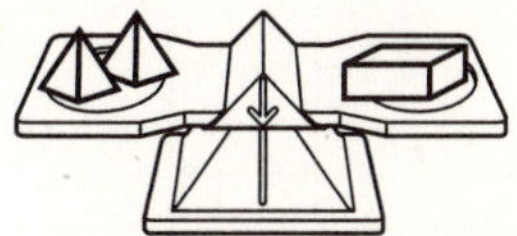

triangular box, rectangular box,

cylinder

STRETCH YOUR THINKING   E117

Connect the Dots

Graph the ordered pairs in the order given. Connect them to reveal a figure.

Start: $(^-2,13)$, $(^-3,14)$, $(^-4,16)$, $(^-3,17)$, $(^-1,17)$, $(0,16)$, $(1,14)$, $(1,13)$, $(5,14)$, $(9,14)$, $(11,13)$, $(11,11)$, $(12,12)$, $(14,12)$, $(15,11)$, $(15,7)$, $(14,6)$, $(13,7)$, $(11,7)$, $(11,^-1)$, $(12,0)$, $(14,0)$, $(15,^-1)$, $(15,^-5)$, $(14,^-6)$, $(13,^-5)$, $(11,^-5)$, $(11,^-6)$, $(9,^-9)$, $(9,^-17)$, $(8,^-19)$, $(6,^-19)$, $(6,^-20)$, $(4,^-20)$, $(2,^-19)$, $(^-4,^-17)$, $(^-4,^-13)$, $(^-12,^-14)$, $(^-4,^-9)$, $(^-12,^-7)$, $(^-7,^-5)$, $(^-9,0)$, $(^-9,9)$, $(^-5,13)$, $(^-2,13)$ Stop!

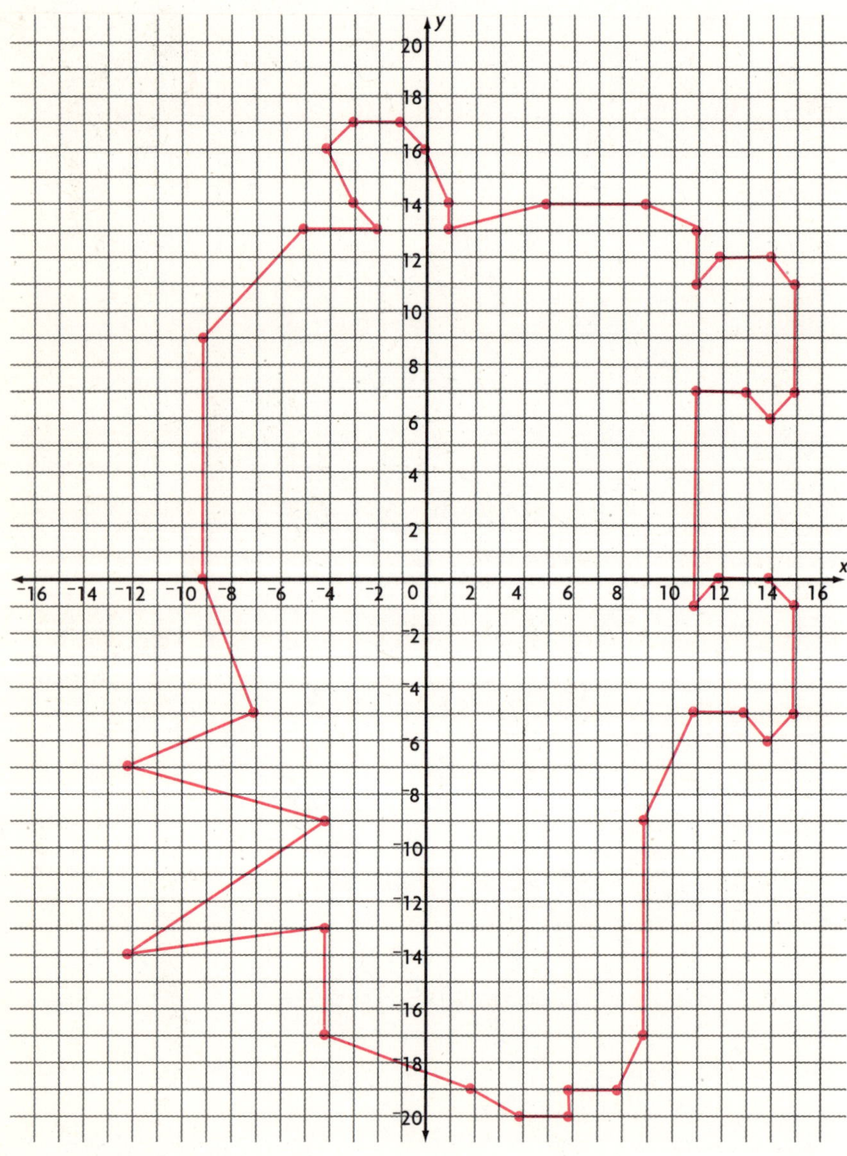

What is the figure?

<u>   **a rabbit**   </u>

Math-Ball Machines

These are special gum-ball machines. When you put money in, you are
never sure what will come out. Examine each picture to determine
what will come out in the last picture.

1.

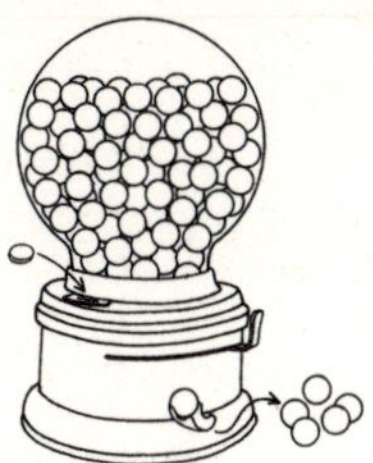 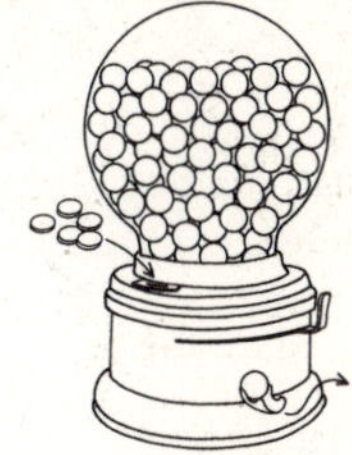

_________________ **9 gum balls**

2.

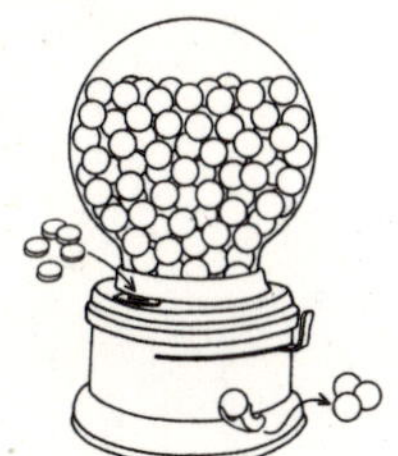  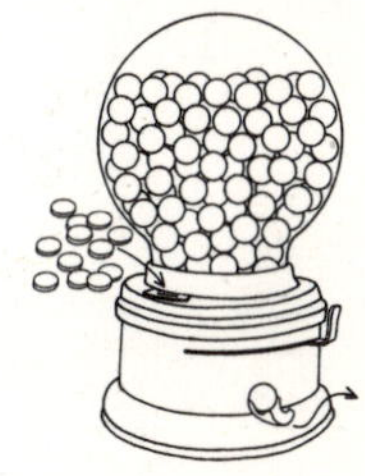

_________________ **10 gum balls**

3.

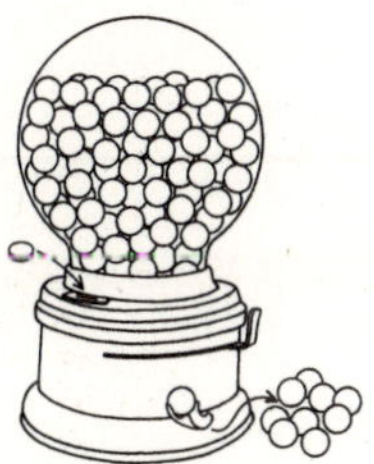 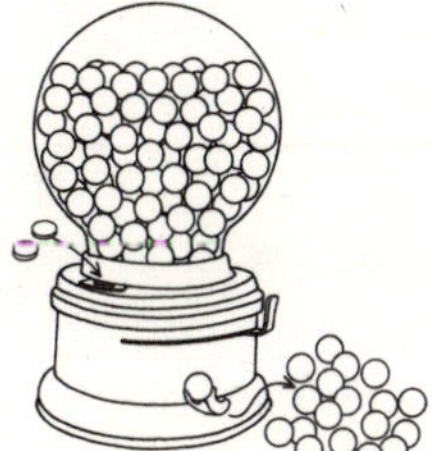  

_________________ **27 gum balls**

4.

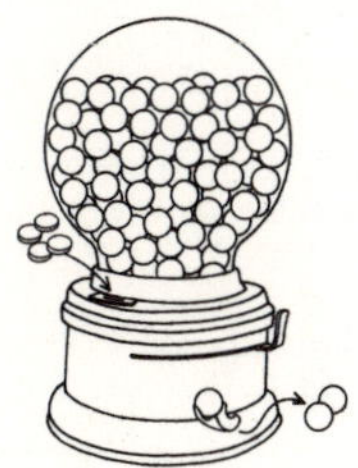 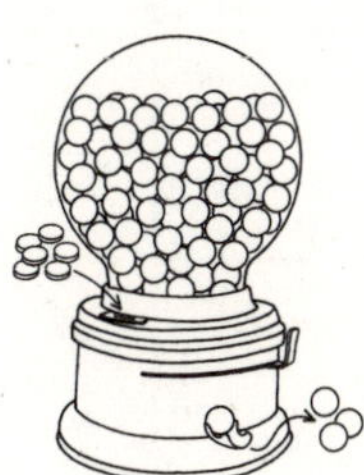 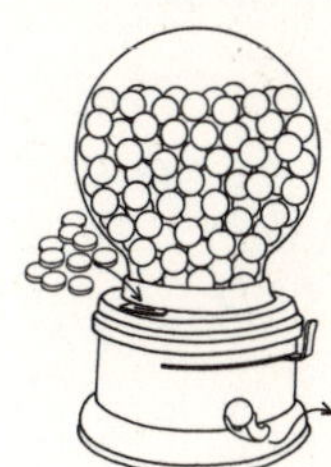

_________________ **5 gum balls**

STRETCH YOUR THINKING   E119

It's All in the Translation

The endpoints of 12 line segments are given. Translate each segment as indicated. On the graph below, draw the translation of each segment. Do not draw the original segments. The translations will make a word.

Endpoints	Translation	Endpoints	Translation
1. (3,5), (3,⁻1)	down 1	7. (⁻9,0), (⁻12,6)	down 2, left 1
2. (6,0), (6,⁻6)	up 4	8. (0,0), (⁻3,⁻6)	up 4, left 7
3. (10,8), (10,2)	down 4	9. (⁻6,0), (⁻3,6)	down 2
4. (⁻10,⁻2), (⁻10,4)	left 3	10. (0,4), (3,⁻2)	left 3
5. (0,8), (0,2)	down 4, left 7	11. (⁻4,8), (0,8)	down 4, right 5
6. (⁻5,⁻5), (⁻1,⁻5)	up 5	12. (6,7), (10,7)	down 7

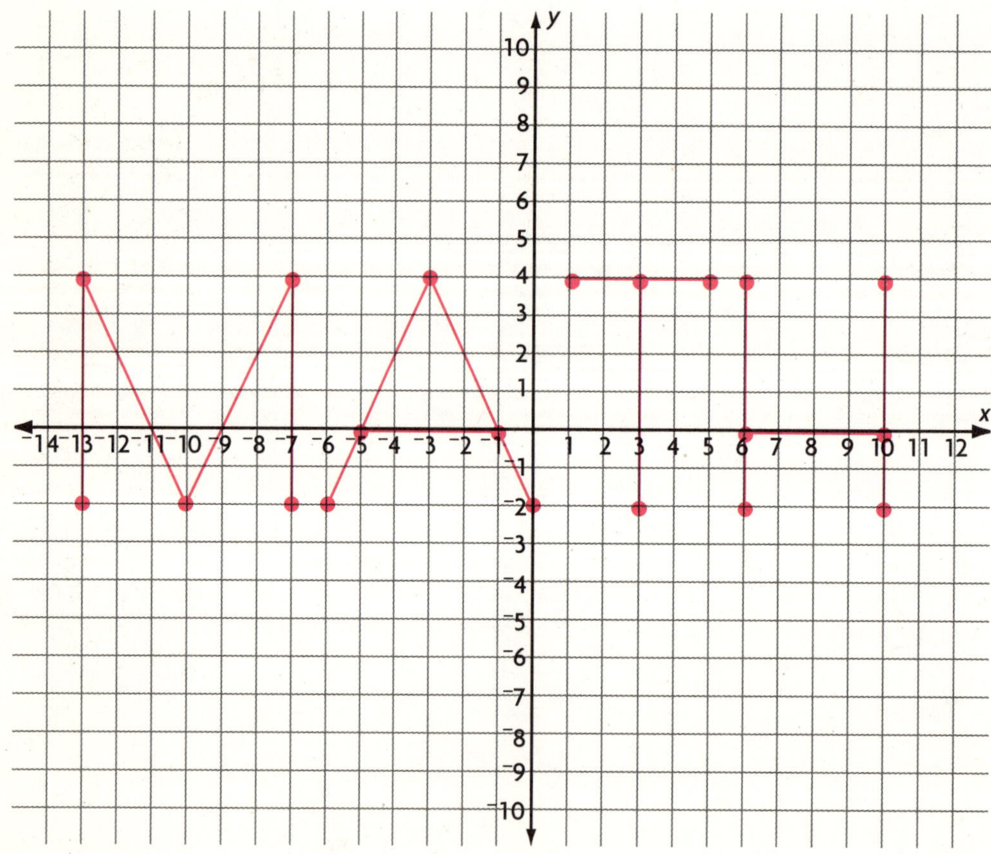

Transformations in Everyday Life

Here are some real-life examples of transformations. Answer the questions about them. Compare your answers with those of your classmates.

Translations

You move the sofa into the corner of the living room as shown. This is a translation.

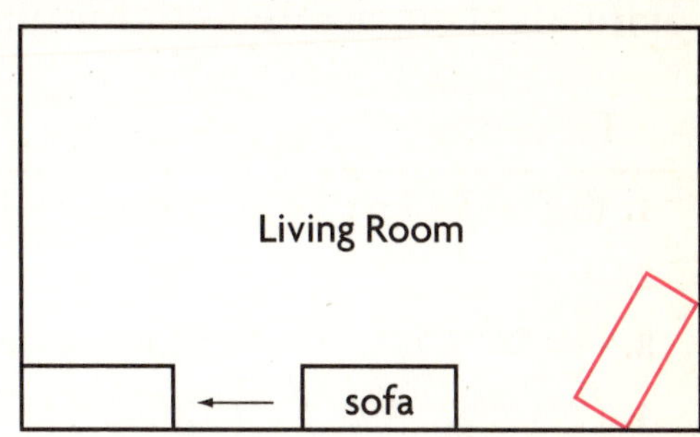

1. Draw a new position for the sofa that would *not* be an example of a translation. **Sample answer is shown.**

2. If you move the sofa directly across the room and position it against the opposite wall, is this a translation? Explain.

   No. To be of use there, the sofa would have to be rotated

   so that you can sit in it and face the center of the room.

Reflections

A stop sign, when viewed from the back, has a left side and a right side separated by an imaginary line down the center. The left side is the reflection of the right side.

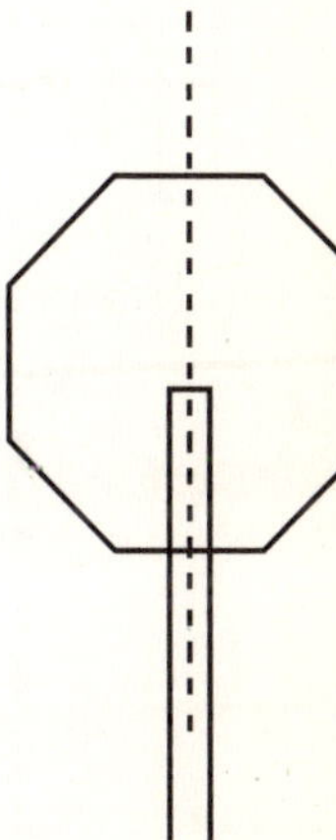

3. Draw a stop sign viewed from the front. Is the left side a reflection of the right side? Explain.

   no, because of the letters *S, T, O*, and *P*

4. Describe at least two other everyday examples of reflection.

   Answers will vary. Samples: reflections in a mirror;

   a snowflake design in which the left side is a

   reflection of the right side

Rotations

The movements of the hands on a clock are examples of clockwise rotation.

5. The big hand rotates how many times faster than the little hand?

   12 times

6. Describe at least two other everyday examples of rotation.

   Answers will vary. Samples: a lawn sprinkler; a CD when it is being played.

STRETCH YOUR THINKING   E121

LESSON 27.3

What's the Score?

A scoreboard may use rectangular patterns
of lights to form numbers and letters.

At the right are 8 × 10 grids forming a 7 and an *A*.

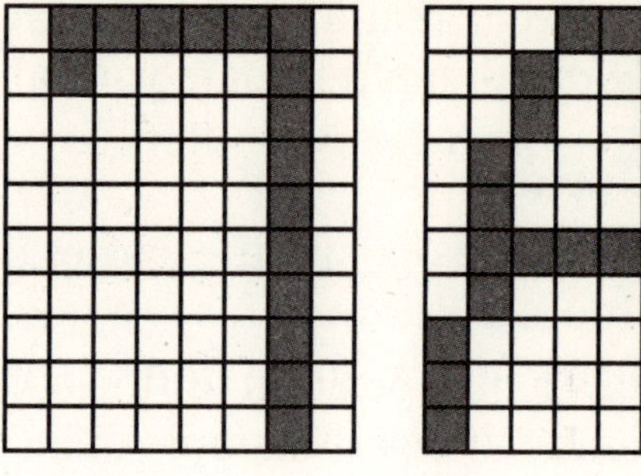

1. On the grids below, give the score of a Bulls-Knicks
   basketball game. Form the numbers by shading patterns
   on the 8 × 10 grids. **Answers will vary.**

Chicago Bulls   New York Knicks

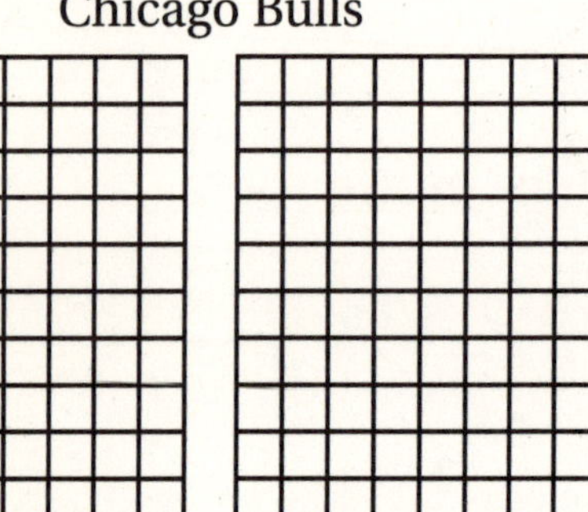
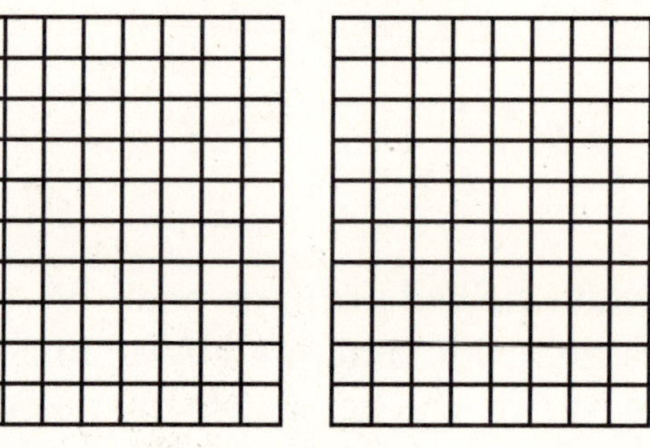

2. On the grid below, write your first or last name using patterns.
   Experiment! **Check students' work.**

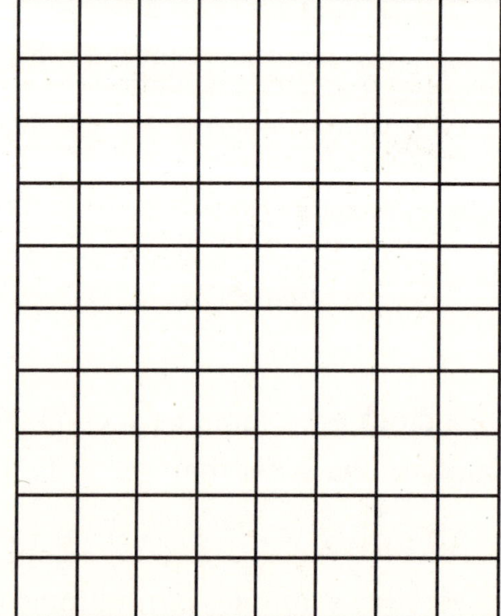

E122   STRETCH YOUR THINKING

Be an Artist

M. C. Escher, a Dutch artist, used tessellations in his artwork. You might wish to research his work and show the class some examples.

You, too, can be an "Escher"! Here's how.

- Cut out a square that is 2 in. × 2 in.

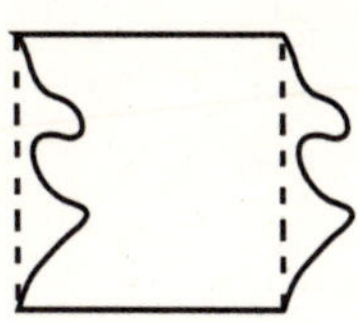

- Mark any design, going from one corner to the next.

- Cut out that design, and slide it to the opposite side. Then tape it.

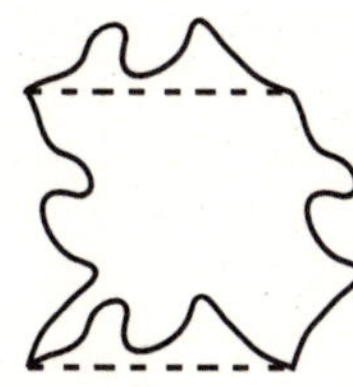

- Repeat the process, using the other two sides.

- Rotate the final piece if you wish, and tessellate.

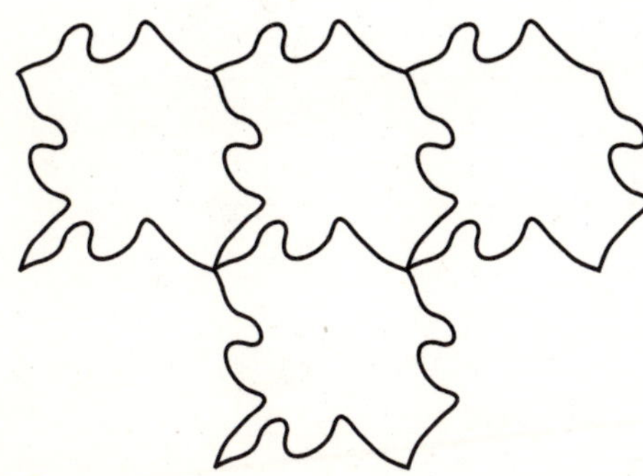

In the space below, create your own Escher-like tessellation.

Check students' tessellations.

Operation 42

Each circle has four numbers. If you perform three different operations on them, the final result is 42. The first one has been done for you.

1. 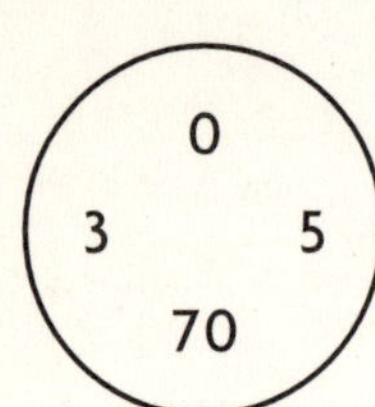

A. $70 \div 5 = 14$

B. $14 \times 3 = 42$

C. $42 - 0 = 42$

2. 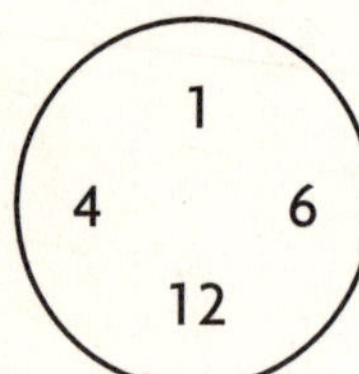

A. $12 \times 4 = 48$

B. $48 - 6 = 42$

C. $42 \div 1 = 42$

3. 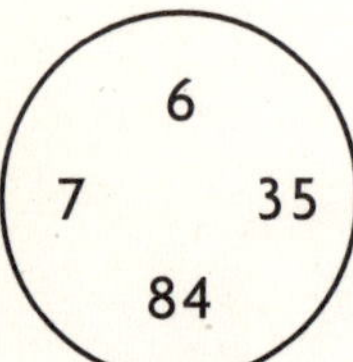

A. $84 \div 6 = 14$

B. $14 + 35 = 49$

C. $49 - 7 = 42$

4. 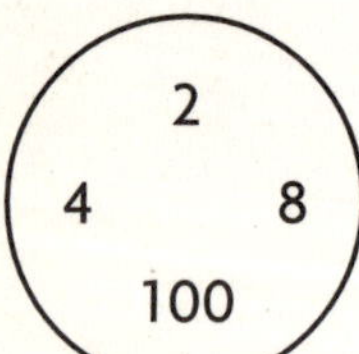

A. $100 \div 4 = 25$

B. $25 \times 2 = 50$

C. $50 - 8 = 42$

5. 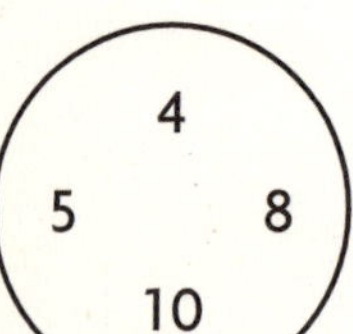

A. $30 \div 5 = 6$

B. $6 \times 7 = 42$

C. $42 - 0 = 42$

6. 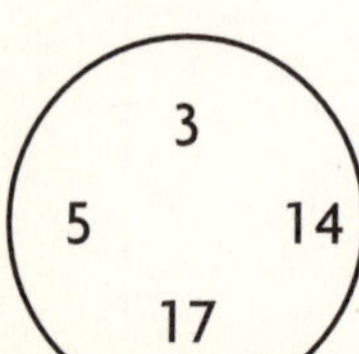

A. $5 + 8 = 13$

B. $13 \times 4 = 52$

C. $52 - 10 = 42$

7.

A. $17 \times 3 = 51$

B. $51 - 14 = 37$

C. $37 + 5 = 42$

Fraction Patterns

Each pattern below alternates between fractions and decimals. Follow
this format to find the next three terms. Then write the rule used to
form the pattern. The first one has been done for you.

1. $\frac{9}{10}$, 1.15, $1\frac{2}{5}$, _____ 1.65 _____ , _____ $1\frac{9}{10}$ _____ , _____ 2.15 _____

Rule: _____ Add $\frac{1}{4}$, or 0.25, to the previous term. _____

2. 1.6, $2\frac{2}{5}$, 3.2, _____ 4 _____ , _____ 4.8 _____ , _____ $5\frac{3}{5}$ _____

Rule: _____ Add $\frac{4}{5}$, or 0.8, to the previous term. _____

3. $7\frac{1}{2}$, 6.9, $6\frac{3}{10}$, _____ 5.7 _____ , _____ $5\frac{1}{10}$ _____ , _____ 4.5 _____

Rule: _____ Subtract $\frac{3}{5}$, or 0.6, from the previous term. _____

4. 9.5, $8\frac{4}{5}$, 8.1, _____ $7\frac{2}{5}$ _____ , _____ 6.7 _____ , _____ 6 _____

Rule: _____ Subtract $\frac{7}{10}$, or 0.7, from the previous term. _____

5. $1\frac{1}{4}$, 1.6, $1\frac{19}{20}$, _____ 2.3 _____ , _____ $2\frac{13}{20}$ _____ , _____ 3 _____

Rule: _____ Add $\frac{35}{100}$, or 0.35, to the previous term. _____

6. 5.75, $5\frac{3}{5}$, 5.45, _____ $5\frac{3}{10}$ _____ , _____ 5.15 _____ , _____ 5 _____

Rule: _____ Subtract $\frac{15}{100}$, or 0.15, from the previous term. _____

7. 9.25, $9\frac{2}{10}$, 9.15, _____ $9\frac{1}{10}$ _____ , _____ 9.05 _____ , _____ 9 _____

Rule: _____ Subtract $\frac{5}{100}$, or 0.05, from the previous term. _____

8. 13.8, $14\frac{1}{5}$, 14.6, _____ 15 _____ , _____ 15.4 _____ , _____ $15\frac{4}{5}$ _____

Rule: _____ Add $\frac{4}{10}$, or 0.4, to the previous term. _____

9. $3\frac{1}{5}$, 3.6, 4, _____ 4.4 _____ , _____ $4\frac{4}{5}$ _____ , _____ 5.2 _____

Rule: _____ Add $\frac{2}{5}$, or 0.4, to the previous term. _____

10. $6\frac{1}{8}$, 6.875, $7\frac{5}{8}$, _____ 8.375 _____ , _____ $9\frac{1}{8}$ _____ , _____ 9.875 _____

Rule: _____ Add $\frac{3}{4}$, or 0.75, to the previous term. _____

Multiply to Solve!

Match each sequence in Column 1 with its fourth term in Column 2.
Write each corresponding letter on the lines below marked with the
exercise number to solve the puzzle.

Column 1

F ___ 1. $\frac{3}{7}, \frac{3}{14}, \frac{3}{28}, \ldots$

L ___ 2. $\frac{4}{5}, \frac{2}{5}, \frac{1}{5}, \ldots$

A ___ 3. $\frac{7}{10}, \frac{7}{15}, \frac{14}{45}, \ldots$

P ___ 4. $2\frac{1}{4}, 1\frac{1}{2}, 1, \ldots$

W ___ 5. $1\frac{4}{5}, \frac{9}{10}, \frac{9}{20}, \ldots$

D ___ 6. $\frac{8}{9}, 1\frac{7}{9}, 3\frac{5}{9}, \ldots$

N ___ 7. $\frac{3}{10}, 1\frac{1}{2}, 7\frac{1}{2}, \ldots$

C ___ 8. $\frac{4}{7}, 4, 28, \ldots$

T ___ 9. $3\frac{1}{3}, \frac{2}{3}, \frac{2}{15}, \ldots$

H ___ 10. $\frac{9}{10}, 2\frac{7}{10}, 8\frac{1}{10}, \ldots$

S ___ 11. $\frac{3}{5}, \frac{3}{50}, \frac{3}{500}, \ldots$

E ___ 12. $\frac{5}{6}, 1\frac{2}{3}, 3\frac{1}{3}, \ldots$

O ___ 13. $\frac{5}{8}, 2\frac{1}{2}, 10, \ldots$

R ___ 14. $\frac{6}{7}, 1\frac{5}{7}, 3\frac{3}{7}, \ldots$

U ___ 15. $\frac{4}{9}, 4, 36, \ldots$

I ___ 16. $\frac{1}{10}, \frac{1}{20}, \frac{1}{40}, \ldots$

Column 2

A. $\frac{28}{135}$

C. 196

D. $7\frac{1}{9}$

E. $6\frac{2}{3}$

F. $\frac{3}{56}$

H. $24\frac{3}{10}$

I. $\frac{1}{80}$

L. $\frac{1}{10}$

N. $37\frac{1}{2}$

O. 40

P. $\frac{2}{3}$

R. $6\frac{6}{7}$

S. $\frac{3}{5,000}$

T. $\frac{2}{75}$

U. 324

W. $\frac{9}{40}$

T H E   P R O D U C T
9   10   12   4   14   13   6   15   8   9

O F   T W O   F R A C T I O N S
13   1   9   5   13   1   14   3   8   9   16   13   7   11

I S   L E S S   T H A N
16   11   2   12   11   11   9   10   3   7

E I T H E R   F A C T O R
12   16   9   10   12   14   1   3   8   9   13   14

E126   STRETCH YOUR THINKING

Operations with Integers

Each diamond has four integers. If you perform three different
operations on these integers, you will produce the underlined
amount. The first one has been done for you.

1. 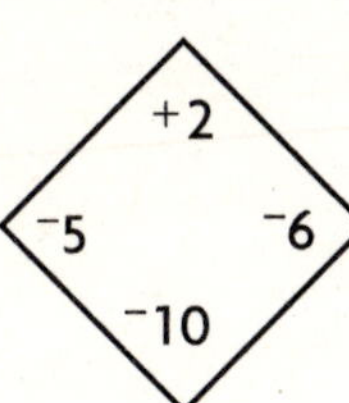

$+35$

A. $^-10 \div (^+2) = ^-5$

B. $^-5 \times (^-6) = ^+30$

C. $^+30 - (^-5) = ^+35$

2. 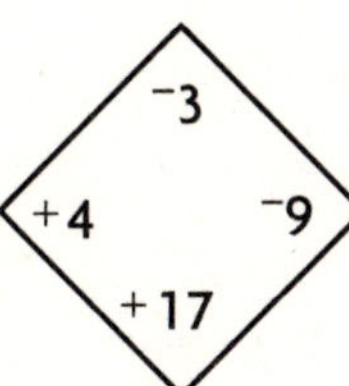

$^-15$

A. $^+17 \times (^-3) = ^-51$

B. $^-51 + (^-9) = ^-60$

C. $^-60 \div (^+4) = ^-15$

3. 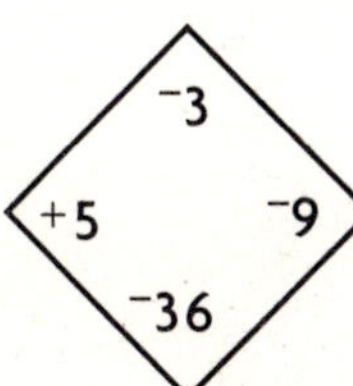

$+17$

A. $^-36 \div (^-9) = ^+4$

B. $^+4 \times (^+5) = ^+20$

C. $^+20 + (^-3) = ^+17$

4. 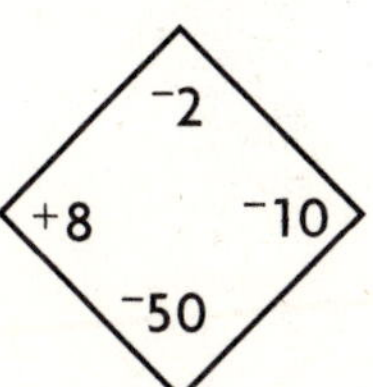

$^-2$

A. $^-50 \times (^-2) = ^+100$

B. $^+100 \div (^-10) = ^-10$

C. $^-10 + (^+8) = ^-2$

5. 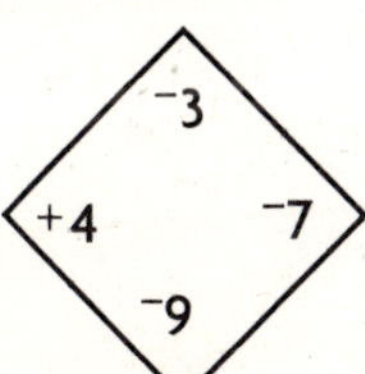

$^-17$

A. $^-7 \times (^-9) = ^+63$

B. $^+63 \div (^-3) = ^-21$

C. $^-21 + (^+4) = ^-17$

6. 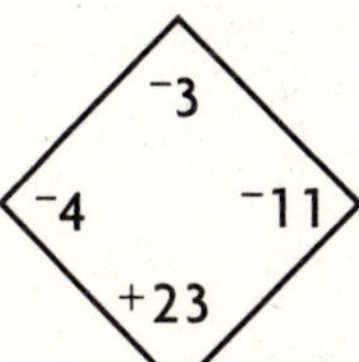

$^-51$

A. $^-11 + (^+23) = ^+12$

B. $^+12 \times (^-4) = ^-48$

C. $^-48 + (^-3) = ^-51$

7.

0

A. $^-9 \times (^+5) = ^-45$

B. $^-45 \div (^+15) = ^-3$

C. $^-3 + (^+3) = 0$

STRETCH YOUR THINKING   E127